PHIL
AS AN AP
THE SPIRIT

An Introduction to the Fundamental Works
of Rudolf Steiner

RICHARD SEDDON

TEMPLE LODGE

Temple Lodge Publishing
Hillside House, The Square
Forest Row, RH18 5ES

www.templelodge.com

Published by Temple Lodge 2005

A catalogue record for this book is available from the British Library

ISBN 1 902636 69 4

Cover by Andrew Morgan featuring a photograph of Rudolf Steiner as a young man
Typeset by DP Photosetting, Aylesbury, Bucks.
Printed and bound by Cromwell Press Limited, Trowbridge, Wilts.

Contents

Preface

The object of this study is to outline the whole range of the purely philosophical work of Dr Rudolf Steiner (1861–1925) as straightforwardly as possible for those hitherto unacquainted with his philosophy. He once wrote, 'I am of the opinion that we best characterize greatness when we attempt to portray it in all its monumental simplicity.'*

When he originally presented these views he naturally had to defend them against those of his contemporaries, and they present difficulties to non-philosophers of today. His views were too far in advance of the age to be recognized, and are virtually unknown to modern philosophers. In the new millennium, however, when his later works of spiritual science (anthroposophy) based on them are gaining increasing recognition, they need to be widely understood. Since this philosophy is a description of his living experiences, it is here set in the context of a brief biography selected to show how it developed. Quotations from his autobiography become elucidated in what follows.

The possibility of interweaving the conclusions of several works into a single train of thought arises from the fact that each contains the germs from which the next develops. This inner consistency is an outstanding characteristic of all Rudolf Steiner's work. Trained thinkers will forgive the resulting repetitions, which those new to philosophy may find helpful.

Extracts, generally in précis, are taken from the original

---

* *Goethe's Conception of the World.*

translations, as they are generally more literal than current versions. The text is limited (with the important exception of the nature of perception) to the positive considerations Steiner advances; anyone who wishes to disagree will need to read the original works, where many possible objections are already raised and answered. Italics, including the overview after each philosophical section, are mainly due to the editor, but include those of Steiner himself.

What was important for Steiner was less the body of his ideas themselves than the transformation they can bring about in the reader by opening the mind to the real nature of the spiritual world. Philosophy, properly regarded, is not the intellectual solution of abstract questions not being asked, but an activity that helps to resolve the questions that arise in the course of life itself. It must therefore itself become organically alive. I am acutely aware that a skeleton such as this formed from the dry bones of several organisms gives scant indication of these organisms in the fullness of life. May it serve however as an introduction to the latter, and to the fullness of anthroposophy in which the power of Christ becomes visible.

It is possible to watch here with admiration the struggles of a great man against the false conceptions of his time, many of which are still prevalent today, as part of a great battle between the redemptive powers of Christ and those of the adversary forces. Only when others come to feel these struggles as their own can his stature be adequately recognized.

I am most grateful to my wife Mary for giving me time to prepare this text whilst she is unwell, to Nick Thomas for advice on atomic particles, and to Sharman Wagstaff for keyboarding, including my many adjustments. Special thanks are due to members of our local anthroposophical study group, who have bravely worked through these pages in draft, made plain where clarifications were required, and suggested a 'punch line' at the end of each section.

Finally I must express my appreciation of a substantial grant from the Anthroposophical Society in Great Britain and further support from the Hermes Trust, the Rudolf Steiner Association and friends, which have made this publication possible.

Richard Seddon, March 2005

PART ONE—BIOGRAPHICAL
(TO AGE 27)

1. Childhood (1861–7)

From the first hour of his life Rudolf Steiner was surrounded by the most recent achievements of civilization—the railway and telegraph—for his father was a railway telegraphist living in the local station. He was born of Austrian peasant parentage, but on the border of Hungary and Croatia, a Slav region, and said later: 'I couldn't be a Central European.'

When he was two his father was moved to the foot of the Austrian Snow Mountain amidst the beauties of nature. From here he could see in the blue distance the Styrian Mountains glistening in the sunshine and frequently covered by the most wonderful snowfields. But his affection for this was constantly overshadowed by a very deep interest in everything of a mechanical character around him, and he would imitate everything that his father did.

His father soon withdrew him from the local school and taught him in the station office, without kindling any real interest. But he quickly learned to write, and was very curious about the elasticity of the quill, and how the dust dried that was used to blot the ink. There was a new spinning mill in the village where he was welcomed, and he studied with all his heart the work of the miller. But he was not allowed into the yarn factory, and what went on between the incoming raw material and the outgoing product was an insoluble problem. 'It is no good asking questions where you can't see.' When a freight wagon caught fire he was long absorbed in how this could happen. Nearby was a mountain railway that brought visitors from Vienna with whom he came in contact. All this left a deep mark on him and drew out his forces.

His family were 'outsiders' and his father was a freethinker. Since the village priest was a comical character, and the priest from the next village who often visited the family spoke of anything but what ordinarily interests a priest, this led to a natural indifference to religion. He showed a very marked individuality and an inborn sense of freedom—rather than do what he did not agree with, such as greet his father's superiors, he hid in the waiting room. He loved to penetrate the mysteries of a picture book with moveable figures.[1]

2. Boyhood (1868–74)

While still seven, young Rudolf was alone in the waiting room when he noticed the door open and a woman enter, which he found quite natural. He had never seen her before, but she was very like his family. Coming to the centre of the room she gestured and said something like, 'Try now and later in life to help me as much as you can.' After further gestures that he could never forget she went to the stove and disappeared into it. This event naturally made a great impression on the boy, but he knew there was no one he could speak to about it without a severe scolding. It soon transpired that a close relative living far away, whom he had never met or heard much about, had committed suicide at that very hour.[2]

From then on a different soul life began to develop: 'I lived together with the spirits of nature that can be especially observed in such a region, the creative beings behind the objects, and submitted to their influence in the same way as to that of the external world.' 'I had two conceptions which were naturally undefined but which played a great role in my life, even before I was seven: I distinguished those things "which are seen" from those "which are not seen". For the reality of the spiritual was to me as certain as that of the physical.'

His father was moved that year to Neudorfl on the border with Austria. At school Rudolf revealed a talent for drawing, and in the teacher's room found a book on geometry, 'That we can live with the mind in the shaping of forms perceived only within ourselves, entirely without impression upon the external sense—this gave me the deepest satisfaction ... With regard to geometry I said to myself: here one is permitted to know something which the mind alone, through its own power, experiences. There exists a sort of soul space, which is the arena of spiritual realities and occurrences. Moreover, this is how to carry knowledge of "things which are not seen".' That was a world in which he loved to live.

He did not learn much in religion, but when he was ten the priest spoke of the Copernican system and the movements of the sun, moon and earth, all of which he was well able to grasp—'I directed all my search for knowledge to this.' He took his turn assisting the priest at Mass (though his father soon stopped this) and in the solemnity of the Latin and Liturgy his soul found a vital happiness, for the Liturgy was for him a profound experience mediating between things 'seen' and 'not seen'.

A doctor visited his home who introduced him enthusiastically to German literature. In reading, his mind went immediately to the concepts and ideas; but in writing he went for the sounds as spoken in dialect, and had to make the greatest effort to spell and formulate correctly.[3]

At the age of eleven he was sent to the Realschule (Technical Modern School) in Wiener Neustadt with a view to becoming a civil engineer. This involved crossing the border by train and an hour's walk home across fields, often deep in snow, to which he later ascribed his excellent health. He had a first-rate geometry teacher who led him on to descriptive geometry and geometrical drawing. From his third year he also had an enthusiastic teacher of mathematics and physics whose clear, methodical and exact thinking became a model for his own. With the help of self-instruction books, he taught himself sufficient calculus, trigonometry and probability theory to understand mathematical essays written by his teacher and the headmaster, which gave him great joy. He also learned shorthand and bookbinding.[4]

3. Youth (1875–81)

By the time he was 14 Rudolf had the feeling 'We can take the right attitude towards experience of the spiritual world only when our process of thinking can attain to the reality of natural phenomena. I must go to nature to win a standpoint in the spiritual world.' 'It seemed to me that thinking could be developed to lay hold upon the things and events of the world ... whatever is in things, this must also be inside human thought.' 'In the first place I wished to build up every thought so that it should be completely subject to survey, that no vague feeling should incline it in any direction whatever. Secondly, I wished to establish a harmony between such thinking and the teachings of religion. I then held quite uncritically to Kant, but no advance did I make by means of him.'

To help his family support his education he tutored pupils of the same or lower grade from this time onwards. This enlivened his thinking and woke up for him what he received in a more dreamy way in the classroom. He already had to consider just what his pupils found difficult to grasp, a practical experience of soul development. When he was 15 religion lessons became voluntary and he gave them up. He was never confirmed—the supersensible world was for him not belief but perception.

Others helped to stimulate him. The doctor who had introduced him to literature lent him books and checked his impressions. His chemistry teacher demonstrated how processes of nature speak for themselves through experiments. When taught Greek and Latin poets in translation he bought textbooks and taught himself both languages. Teachers of history and geography fired him with enthusiasm. And during his last years at school he read as much philosophy as he possibly could.[5]

The year 1879, when he became 18, had great significance in his life. 'My strivings after conceptions in natural science had finally brought me to see in the activity of the human ego the sole starting point for true knowledge. When the ego is active and itself perceives this activity we have something spiritual immediately present in consciousness. [Section 6.] To express this in clear, vivid concepts I devoted myself to Fichte's *Wissenschaftslere* (Theory of Science). And yet I had my own opinions, so I took his volume and rewrote it page by page. There was for me a world of spiritual beings. That the ego, itself spirit, lives in a world of spirits was a matter of direct perception. But nature would not pass over into this spirit world of my experience.'

Steiner was such an excellent scholar that his father was moved to a Vienna suburb to enable him to attend the Technical College, which also entitled him to attend lectures at the University. He enrolled for mathematics, physics and chemistry. Lectures of two professors of philosophy, Zimmerman and Brentano, challenged his thinking, although they did not satisfy. But Schroer, who lectured on German literature and especially on Goethe, impressed him deeply and a 'fatherly' friendship developed.

By now the spiritual individuality of everyone revealed itself to him in clear vision. It united with the physical germ from the parents; and he could follow it on its way after death into the spiritual world. But no one would pay attention if he mentioned such things. And when they spoke of spiritualism, he would have nothing to do with it. So, it was a lonely path.[6]

Then he met on the daily train a man who had similar experiences, with whom he could speak. This was a simple herb-gatherer, who had penetrated deeply into mystical occult wisdom. He loved everything in the world (except clerics) and could explain the occult background of every plant. It was as if he were a soul of ancient times, a mouthpiece for a spiritual content which desired to utter itself out of hidden sources. Through him Steiner met another personality, who stimulated his soul to the regular, systematic path of knowing which we must have for real knowledge of the spiritual worlds. The latter connected the work of Fichte with observations which later became the seeds of the book *Esoteric Science*. And he impressed on Steiner that 'you will only conquer the dragon if you slip within its skin'.[7]

Steiner consequently resolved to enter deeply into the thinking of natural science. His problem now was how to penetrate from the ego as spirit into nature's process of becoming. Can we prove that in thinking real spirit is active? Can we express in thought the immediate vision of the spiritual world?[8]

He made many friends among the students, for a short time acting as treasurer of the students' club, for longer as its librarian (soliciting many books from their authors, which he read avidly) and latterly as president of its reading club. He extended his studies to zoology, botany, biology, geology, geometry, pure mechanics, even medicine. But mathematics remained the most important, because its concepts were reached independently of any external impressions, yet when carried into sense-reality revealed its laws.[9] The concept of space gave him great difficulty, but the thought that the straight line returns on itself came as a revelation. Time however remained a riddle, and current ideas of Darwinism and of the world as motion-events in matter caused him unspeakable difficulties, because they were impossible to relate to his inner experience. Nor could he relate the philosophies he was taught to his perception of the spiritual world.

He began to see thought as a reflection of the reality which was experienced in the spiritual world. The question arose: is the world of the senses in fact a reality complete in itself? (Section 8.) Thought appears to be the means by which that world expresses its own nature, but do we then bring something foreign to it? Before forming his own view he turned to study Hegel. But Hegel led only to a thought world, albeit a living one, not to perception of actual spirit; though the assurance of his thinking was encouraging.[10]

4. Vienna (1882–8)

While he was 21 Steiner was stirred by Schiller's *Letters on Aesthetic Education*. This compares the compulsion of consciousness by sense-experiences with that by logic and reason, and asserts an intermediate aesthetic mood, where in free play one can experience and produce works of beauty in which the true human being comes to life. 'Might one not also think of a state of consciousness that would mediate truth in the being of things? . . . I believed that I knew such a state, when one has thoughts such that one *experiences* them as thoughts. This "living in thoughts" is quite different from the way one ordinarily exists and carries on scientific research ... One penetrates deeper into the thought-life and finds that spiritual reality comes to meet it. One then takes the path of the soul into the spirit. But on this inner way one arrives at a spiritual reality which one finds again within nature . . . such a spiritual perception is comparable in thoroughness to mathematics.' (Section 10.)

The problem of the relation between the inner and outer worlds thus came before him in a new form. He received much spiritual warmth and support from visits to Schroer, a Platonist who held that life was in the idea itself. But for himself it was not so, it was rather that the mind perceives the idea on the spiritual object as the eye perceives colour on a physical object. 'I held strongly to this: to read the facts of nature rightly.' A thesis of this time contains the core of his later thoughts: 'Concepts and laws are always of a general, sense-objects of a particular nature; the former can only be thought, the latter only perceived. Cognition can only mean to merge what is offered to our senses into the universality of the concept world. We have to allow the concept its originality and apprehend it *in* the perceptible object, only in a different form.' (Section 8.)

Although colour only manifests when an obstruction hinders light, the light itself does not exist in the sense world, only as a midway stage between sense-perceptible realities and realities visible to the spirit (Section 18). The world of pure musical tone-forms, too, is the revelation of an essential aspect of reality which has content in itself, not merely through the percept (the notes). And in the realm of soul, he saw in thinking, feeling and will the living manifestation of creative forces that set the human being as spirit before him, completing the sense-manifestation by a spirit-form ruling in the supersensible.

He thus came upon the *sensible-supersensible form* which thrusts itself, both for true vision of nature and for spirit vision, *between* what the senses grasp and what the spirit perceives. He was freed from his hesitation about this through Goethe's famous conversation with Schiller in which he outlined his 'archetypal plant' (Section 13). This represents the totality of the plant by a supersensible form out of which leaf, blossom etc. shape themselves to reproduce, in detail, the whole. Schiller could only regard this totality as an idea, whereas Goethe saw the whole spiritually, as much a part of reality as the details of a moment, saying that in that case he perceived his ideas with his eyes.[11]

After finishing at Technical College, where he lived by tutoring not only in mathematics and physics but even in bookkeeping, Steiner became resident tutor to a Jewish family with four boys. The youngest was a hydrocephalic, from the study of whose needs he gained a knowledge of the human being which he could not have developed so vitally in any other way—moreover Steiner himself learned for the first time how to play! He enabled this boy and one brother to attend the Gymnasium, for which purpose he taught himself the classical curriculum. The other two he tutored for the Technical Modern School.

This task left him enough time to accept an offer (thanks to Schroer) to edit Goethe's scientific writings for the Kürschner edition. The first volume* appeared in 1885 when he was 24. But before continuing he found it necessary to write *The Theory of Knowledge Implicit in Goethe's World Conception.* This was his first philosophical work, which appeared in 1886.[†] He then went on to complete the second volume of Goethe's writings[‡] in which his ideas were developed further.[12] Indeed it was about this time that the thoughts for his later work *The Philosophy of Freedom* approached him. 'We should surely finally admit that a being who knows himself cannot be unfree.'[13]

With strong inner concentration he took a wide interest in other people. Even where he was tutoring he and the boys' aunt were aware of love for one another, but neither could say so, and life separated them. He describes his entry into circles of architects, musicians, poets, painters, writers, socialists; and he later spoke of many of them as 'homeless souls' who with their spiritual ambitions no longer felt at home in the mainstream of life.[14] To a Cistercian priest he was able to say that Jesus of Nazareth, by means of supramundane influence, had received Christ into himself, and that Christ has lived as a spiritual being in human evolution since the Mystery of Golgotha.

He also attained at this time to definite views about

---

* See Bibliography.

[†] In an inscription he said of it: 'What stands in this book, I have not merely written, I have lived it. When the powers within me encountered one another in consuming battle I sought to trace in words the course of the wrestling spirit. So take in a friendly way that in the magic of whose words the beauty of the spirit is so grandly unfolded.'

[‡] See Bibliography.

repeated earth lives, for he had gained real perception in this sphere.[15] In 1884/85 he had already met the Theosophical Society and turned away, because the whole behaviour and attitude was not in harmony with scientific exactness.[16] Now he learned to know it thoroughly and was again repelled, especially by a book of Sinnett.[17]

For a short while he edited a journal, *Deutsche Wochenschrift* (German Weekly), writing on public affairs. Yet he felt an impulse to intense spiritual concentration and inner withdrawal. He had come to see the task of artists as the metamorphosis of the soul powers into a pure spiritual perception. 'I desired through a perception of the true to experience the spirit in its own being, whose spiritual reflection is moral conduct, and towards which creative art strives in the shaping of sensible form.' He spoke to the Goethe Society on 'Goethe as Father of a New Aesthetic', describing art as 'the representation of the sense-perceptible in the form of the spirit'.[18] The Goethe Society then invited him to contribute to their complete edition of Goethe's works based on the archive at Weimar, and he spent some weeks there before agreeing.[19]

He regarded this as the completion of the first period of his life. 'Karma works through the struggle of the soul outwards, harmonizing with what comes from the outer world towards us. We do not at first possess our own true being, our genuine self-consciousness, but must first attain to this.' (Section 26.) A visit to Transylvania before moving to Weimar enabled him to educate his perception for the outer world, which had never been easy for him, whereas 'in the element of the spiritual I lived as in something self-evident'.[20]

PART TWO—THEORY OF KNOWLEDGE
(1885–94)

5. Experience

Each branch of science has its sphere in which it seeks for the interrelationships among phenomena. It is the task of a theory of knowledge to clarify the relationship between idea and reality, between the objects of reality and our thoughts about them.[1] Its first task is thus to fix sharply the boundaries of these two spheres, experience and thought.

What is experience? We become aware of an external world of many items very highly complicated, and we live in a more or less richly elaborated inner world. We have no share in its coming to pass, it is as if it sprang forth from an unknown realm, and we can at first only let our look sweep over the multiplicity that meets us. *Pure experience* is that form of reality in which it appears to us when we meet it *with the complete exclusion of ourselves.*

As regards the external senses, this will scarcely be denied by anyone. A body appears at first as a complex of forms, colours, sensations of heat and light which are immediately there. The matter is not so clear in the case of our inner life, but our inner states appear in a similar way. A feeling makes its impact on me as does a sensation—the fact that I bring it into nearer relationship with my own personality has no significance from this point of view. Even thought itself appears to us at first as an item of experience. Everything that is to become an object of knowledge must adapt itself to this form of setting itself before us.[2]

In what does pure experience first consist? It is merely

juxtaposition in space and succession in time; an aggregate of nothing but unrelated single entities. No one of these entities which come and go has anything to do with any other. The world is at this stage a multiplicity of things of uniform importance or unimportance. The single entities must naturally be different from one another, but there is an absolute want of meaning in them.[3]

Must we regard the form in which we have hitherto recognized experience as rooted in the nature of things? Is it a characteristic of reality? Much depends on the answer to this question. If it is an essential characteristic, it is impossible to see how this stage can ever be surmounted. But if this is only its quite inessential external aspect, we should have to surmount this first appearance to unfold out of it a higher form of appearance.[4]

If everything were *merely* given, we should never get beyond the bare gazing outwards into the external world and a no less bare gazing inwards into the privacy of our inner world. We should at most be able to describe, but never to understand, what is outside us. If there is to be knowledge everything depends on there being, somewhere within the given, a field in which our cognitive activity is at work in the very heart of the given. The whole difficulty in understanding knowledge lies in the fact that we do not create the world-content out of ourselves. There must however be a point within the given at which our activity does not float in a vacuum, but where the world-content itself enters into our activity. If there is such a field, knowledge can be explained; if not, not. Our next task is clearly to locate such a point, which must again be done by means of immediate observation rightly directed.[5]

The experience of given data is an aggregate of entities as yet unrelated.

6. *The Activity of Thinking*

Observation and thinking are the two points of departure for all conscious spiritual striving of the human being. The workings of common sense as well as the most complicated scientific researches rest on these two fundamental pillars of our spirit. But thinking as an object of experience differs essentially from all other objects. Its peculiar nature lies just in the fact that it is an activity directed solely on the observed object, and not on the thinking personality. This is apparent even in the way we express our thoughts, as distinct from our feelings and acts of will. We do not usually say, 'I am thinking of a table,' but, 'That is a table,' whereas we do say, 'I like (or want) the table.' This is just the peculiar nature of thinking, that the thinker forgets it whilst actually engaged in it. The first observation that we make about thinking is, therefore, that it is the unobserved element in our ordinary mental and spiritual life.

The reason why we do not observe the thinking in our ordinary life is that it is due to our own activity. Whatever I do not myself produce appears before me as an object; I must accept it as a premiss that precedes my thinking process. While I reflect upon an object I am occupied with it, and to be thus occupied is precisely to contemplate by thinking. I attend not to my activity, but to the object of this activity.

I am moreover in the same position when I enter into the exceptional state and reflect on my own thinking. I can never observe my *present* thinking. I can only subsequently take experiences of my thinking process as the object of fresh thinking. If I wanted to watch my present thinking, I should have to split myself into two persons—one to think and the other to observe it—but this I cannot do. Just because it is my own production I know quite directly the characteristic features of its course, the manner in which the process takes place.* This transparent clearness concerning our thinking process is quite independent of any knowledge of physiological processes. My observation shows me that in linking one thought with another there is nothing to guide me but the *content* of my thoughts; I am not guided by any material processes in the brain.

For everyone who can observe thinking—and with good will every normal person has this ability—this observation is the most important one we can possibly make. For we observe something that we ourselves produce, we know how the thing observed comes into being, and we see into its connections and relationships.

A firm point has now been reached from which we can with some hope of success seek an explanation of all other phenomena. Our investigation only touches firm ground when we find an object which exists in a sense that we can derive from the object itself. But I am myself such an object in that I think, for I give to my existence the definite self-determined content of my thinking activity. While I observe other things there is one process present which is overlooked, namely, my thinking. But when I observe my own thinking there is no such neglected element present; the object of observation is qualitatively identical with the activity directed upon it, I remain within the same element.

This then is indisputable, that *in thinking we have got hold of one corner of the whole world process* which requires our presence if anything is to happen. And this is just the point

* One should not of course confuse the mere 'having of thought images' with the elaboration of thoughts by thinking. (Ed.)

upon which everything turns. The very reason why phenomena confront me at first in such a puzzling way is that I play no part in their production, they are simply given to me; whereas in the case of thinking I know how it is done. Hence for the study of all that happens in the world there can be no more fundamental starting point than thinking itself.[6]

Special attention is drawn to the fact that we make thinking our starting point, not concepts and ideas, which are first gained by means of thinking, and thus presuppose it. Moreover it must not be overlooked that only with the help of thinking can I determine myself as subject and contrast myself with objects. *Therefore thinking must never be regarded as a merely subjective activity.* Thinking lies beyond subject and object, it produces these two concepts just as it produces all others. When as thinker I refer a concept to an object it is not the subject that makes the reference, but thinking. Thinking is thus an element that leads me out beyond myself and connects me with objects, yet at the same time separates me by setting me as subject over against them. It is just this that constitutes our double nature.[7]

Because thinking depends on my activity I am completely aware of it, although I am not in arbitrary control of it.

7. The Content of Thought

Amid the unrelated chaos of experience—and indeed, at first as a fact of experience—we have found an element that leads us out beyond this unrelatedness, namely, thinking.

So long as I limit myself to what is immediately present to the senses, I do not advance beyond the separate units. As regards thinking, such is not the case. If, for example, I grasp the thought of cause, this by its own content leads me to the thought of effect. I need only hold fast to the thoughts in the form in which they enter immediate experience, and they appear as characterizations according to law. A difficulty is thereby resolved which could scarcely be resolved in any other way. It is a justifiable demand that we should limit ourselves to experience, but no less justifiable that we should seek for the inner laws of experience. Therefore this 'inner' must itself appear at some place in experience. We need only take hold of this element of thinking and submerge ourselves in it, for it exists in experience. Through our activity we stand inside it and can really know its very nature. Whereas every external object reveals only its outside to my senses, I know quite certainly that what enters my consciousness as thought is its totality.

Since we experience in thinking alone a real conformity to law, the conformity to law of the rest of experience, which we do not find in this itself, must also lie within thought. In other words, thought and the appearance for the senses are face to face in experience. The latter, however, gives us no disclosure of its essential nature; the former gives us this both as to itself and as to the nature of this appearance for the senses.[8]

It may seem as if we had here introduced the very subjective element we were so determined to exclude, but this rests upon a confusion of two things—the theatre in which our thoughts play their role, and that element from which they derive their content, the inner law of their nature. We do not at all produce a thought *content* in such a way that we determine into what interconnections our thought shall enter. We merely provide the occasion through which the thought content unfolds *according to its own nature*. Our thought world is an entity resting wholly upon itself, a totality self-enclosed, complete and entire within itself. Here we perceive which of the two aspects of the thought world is the essential one: the objective aspect of its content and not its subjective mode of emergence.

We are accustomed to conceive a phenomenon as if we needed only to stand passively before it, observing it. But this is not at all an absolute necessity. No matter how unfamiliar the conception may be to us that by our thought activity we bring an objective entity to manifestation—i.e., that we do not merely become aware of this phenomenon but at the same time produce it—this conception is not at all invalid. It is only necessary that we should abandon the customary idea that there are as many thought worlds as there are human individuals. This idea is nothing more than an ancient pre-conception. It is tacitly presupposed everywhere sub-consciously that another conception is at least equally possible. Let us imagine, in place of the above preconception, that there is one sole thought content, and that our individual thinking is nothing more than an act of working ourselves, our individual personalities, into the thought centre of the world.

From the point of view of its objectivity, the work of the thinker may very appropriately be compared with that of a mechanic. Just as the latter brings natural forces into re-ciprocal action and thus brings about a purposeful activity and exertion of forces, so the thinker causes thought elements to come into reciprocal activity and these evolve into the thought systems which compose our sciences.[9]

How then does this thought world appear when observed in itself? It is a multiplicity of thoughts woven and bound organically together in the most complicated fashion. But all the elements are related one to another, they exist for one another, one modifies another, restricts it and so on. The moment our mind conceives two corresponding thoughts, it observes at once that these really flow together to form a unit. It finds everywhere in its whole realm the interrelated; this concept unites with that, a third illumines or supports a fourth, and so on. All individual thoughts are thus parts of a great whole which we call our conceptual world.

When any single thought emerges in consciousness, I cannot rest until it is brought into harmony with the remainder. Such an isolated concept is entirely unendurable. I am simply conscious that there exists an inwardly sustained harmony among all thoughts, that the thought world is of the nature of a unit. Therefore every such isolation is an abnormality, an untruth. When we have arrived at that state of mind in which our whole thought world bears the character of a complete inner harmony, we gain thereby the satisfaction for which our mind is striving. We feel that we are in possession of truth.[10]

Thinking has however a double function: to form concepts with sharply defined contours, and to unite the single concepts thus formed into a unified whole. We refer to the former as the work of the *intellect*, and the latter as the work of *reason*. Differentiation is a necessary preliminary to all higher forms of knowledge, otherwise the world would appear as a blurred, obscure chaos. But it introduces an artificial multiplicity that has no relation to the essential nature of reality, which is in truth a unity. The *concept* is a single thought as grasped by the intellect. When reason brings together and unites a number of concepts in a living flux, passing over into one another, thought structures arise which we call *ideas*. Reason does not presuppose or contrive the unity between the thoughts concerned, but brings harmony to light where it already exists. All conceptual judgements are nothing more than the reunifying of that which the intellect has divided.

The number of people who have the acumen to differentiate down to the minutest trifles is noticeably greater than those who possess the combining power of reason that penetrates to the depths of the world process.[11]

Thinking relates the single concept objectively to the total world of ideas.

8. Thinking and Perception

Thinking is an organ for observing something higher than is afforded by the senses. A side of reality is accessible to it of which a mere sense-being could never become aware. Thought exists not merely to repeat the sensible, but to penetrate into what is concealed from the senses. *The sense-percept gives us only one side of reality, the other side is the apprehending of the world through thinking.* The thought-characterizations are such that like an equation they may be satisfied in a variety of different ways. The sense-percept affords a means of particularization which is left open by thought itself.

We meet with a specific percept, and it confronts us as a riddle. Within us manifests the impulse to investigate its 'what?'—its real nature—which the percept itself does not express. This impulse is nothing but the upward working of a concept out of the darkness of our consciousness. We then hold this concept firmly, while the sense-percept moves on a parallel line. The mute percept suddenly speaks a language intelligible to us; we know that the concept we took hold of is the real nature of the percept for which we have been seeking. We call this a perceptual judgement.

If we are to comprehend what we perceive, the concept must first be present within us—otherwise we should pass by without the percept being intelligible. Thus people who have lived a rich mental life penetrate far deeper into the world of experience than those who have not. But do we not meet innumerable things in life of which we have not previously had the slightest conception? Of course, but is not my conceptual system capable of evolving? In the presence of a reality unintelligible to me, can I not set my thinking in action to produce on the spot the concept to match the object? I need only possess the capacity to draw a determinate concept out of the store of the thought world accessible to me. Where and when I grasp the concept is not essential to its content.

People are so used to regarding concepts as void of content, in contrast to the world of percepts as filled with content, that it will be difficult for the true facts to win the place belonging to them. The truth is entirely overlooked that mere beholding is the emptiest thing imaginable, and that it receives content only from thinking. The sole truth regarding the object is that it holds the constant flux of thought in a determinate form without our having to cooperate actively in holding it. When one who has a rich mental life sees a thousand things which are nothing to the mentally poor, this shows as clearly as sunlight that the content of reality is only the reflection of the content of our minds, and that we receive from without merely the empty form. Of course, we must possess the inner power to recognize ourselves as the producer of this content; otherwise we shall forever see only the reflection and never our own mind which is reflected. Indeed, one who sees himself in an actual mirror must know himself as a personality in order to recognize himself in the reflected image.

All sense-perception finally resolves itself, as to its *essential* nature, into ideal content. Only then does it appear to us transparent and clear. All sciences should be permeated by the conviction that their content is solely a thought-content, and that they sustain no other relationship to perception than that they see in the perceptual object a specialized form of the concept. To deny thinking the capacity for perceiving in itself entities which are inaccessible to the senses is a denigration of thought.[12]

Nobody supposes that each person has his own stock of colours remaining stuck to the eye after his colour sensations, but there is a peculiar theory that each person has his own thoughts stored up somewhere unexplained below the level of consciousness, to be taken out when needed. Consciousness is not however the ability, having produced thoughts, to store them up, but the ability to perceive them afresh as required. Our mind is not a receptacle for a private world of thoughts, but an organ of perception.[13] *

Truth does not consist in agreement between a mental picture and its object, but expresses a relationship between perceived factors. The connection in idea between perceptual images is not given through the senses but conceived independently by the mind. It does not follow, however, that it is merely subjective; it is the necessary completion of the perceptual image. Thinking does not add to reality; it is neither less nor more an organ of perception than an eye or ear. It perceives ideas, for the idea is not the content of a subjective thinking but the result of research.

Everything depends on how we conceive the relationship

---

* Editor's note: For the occasion when we find the concept that we have been seeking, the English language has coined the accurate word 'insight'. Colloquially we say, 'Aha! I see.'

between idea and sense-perceptible reality. The concept of a triangle is a single one, which embraces all single triangles ever perceived and always remains the same—I have under all circumstances *only one concept 'triangle'*. But within perceptual reality every single thing presents itself as a particular 'this'; and it is confronted by the concept as a rigorous unity, always the same. What then is the source of this identity of the concept? It can only consist in the content of the mental picture, its 'what'.

The particularity of an object cannot be conceived, only perceived. Thus concept and percept confront each other, alike in essence yet different. And since the percept demands the concept, it possesses its essence not in its particularity but in its conceptual universality. This universality however must first be discovered in the subject, for it cannot be gained out of the object. Just as quantities are not found in the concept, so the percept lacks the dynamic, qualitative element of characteristics. To grasp the percept needs only open senses, a passive attitude, whereas the idea-core of the world must arise through the spontaneous procedure of the mind.

What is important is to be aware of what is presented by the senses and what by thinking. Perceptible reality confronts us as ready made; it is simply there like something alien. But we can grasp only that of which we know how it has become. A thought structure does not arise without my participation; I know that I myself have brought it to a finished form. Thus we can finish with a thing only when we have completely penetrated through thinking that which is sensibly perceived, leaving no residue.[14]

The essence of a particular percept lies in the universality of its related idea.

9. The Process of Perception

The word *'percept'* refers to the immediate objects of experience outlined in Section 5 in so far as the conscious subject apprehends them through observation. It is thus not the process of observation but the object of observation. The term 'sensation' is narrower in meaning, because even a feeling in myself becomes known as a percept. Thinking too, in its very first appearance for our consciousness, may be called a percept.

My *percept-picture* changes when I change the place from which I am looking. Thus the form in which this picture presents itself depends on a condition due not to the object but to me—it depends indeed on my whole bodily and spiritual organization as perceiver. That I see a red surface as red depends on the organization of my eye. Percept-pictures are thus in the first instance subjective, and this may lead people to doubt whether there is any objective basis for them at all. This leads us to turn our attention from the object of perception to the subject, the perceiver.

I perceive not only other things but also myself. The percept of myself contains the fact that I am the stable element in the flux of percept-pictures. When I am absorbed in the perception of a tree I am at first aware only of the tree; but to this the percept of myself may be added, so that I know that it is I who see the tree. I know moreover that something happens in me while I am observing the tree, for when it disappears from my sight a picture of it remains in my consciousness. This picture has become associated with my self during my observation. My self has become enriched by a new element. This element is called the 'mental picture' (*Vorstellung*, representation). Only because I perceive my self, and observe that with each percept the content of my self too is changed, am I compelled to speak of my mental pictures. I perceive the mental picture in myself in the same sense as I perceive colour, sound, etc. in other objects. I can now distinguish the objects that confront me as outer world from the percept of my self that I call my inner world.

The failure to recognize the true relationship between the mental picture—a percept of myself as subject—and the percept picture of the object has led to the greatest misunderstandings in modern philosophy. The perception of a change in me has been thrust into the foreground, whilst the object that causes it is lost sight of. It is said that we perceive not objects but only our mental pictures, as though this were self-evident. But it is not so.

This whole view of perception, which derives from Kant and is still almost universally held in the third millennium, may be very briefly summarized as follows. It starts with the thing perceived, none of whose qualities would exist for us if we had no sense organs—no eye, no colour. Therefore the colour is not yet present in the object. But on the path to and in the eye there is supposedly only a chemical-physical process, and much the same is true of the optic nerve and brain. The colour is said to be produced by the brain process, but even then it does not enter consciousness until it has been transferred back to the outer object, where I believe myself to perceive it—a complete circle.

Originally I thought that the colour had objective existence, but here it is interpreted as no more than a mental state. But if this were true, it follows logically that my sense organs, my nerves and my brain are also mere mental states—the whole process becomes nothing but a tissue of mental pictures. But these pictures as such cannot act on one another!

Moreover, there is a gap in the whole argument, for the processes described in eye, optic nerve and brain have no resemblance to the colour I experience; and at the supposed point of transition from physical-chemical brain process to sensation the path of observation is interrupted, with no kind of explanation forthcoming! As soon as I see this clearly, this train of thought reveals itself in its whole absurdity, and it is therefore quite unfitted to explain the process of perception; still less can it be claimed as obvious and needing no proof.[15]

Let us instead look into the facts quite objectively. Assume that we have a sensation of red which calls our attention to some kind of object (we disregard the rare possibility of being struck in the eye). If I ask what spatio-temporal processes occur in the thing while it appears to be red I may discover mechanical, chemical or other occurrences. If I investigate the path from the thing to my sense organs and from there to the brain, nothing can be found as mediator except motion processes or electric currents or chemical changes. What is present on this whole path is the percept red, but how this sensation presents itself in any particular thing on the path depends entirely on the nature of that thing. The sensation itself is present at each place, not as sensation however, not explicit, but in the form corresponding to the nature of the thing. I thus learn nothing more than how the sensation manifests itself in some kind of object of the spatio-temporal world.

Far is it from being true that such a spatial-temporal process is the cause of the sensation released in me. Rather is the opposite true, that the spatial-temporal process is the effect of the sensation in a thing extended in time and space. The sensation is a soul experience which as such I cannot discover in that world, because *it simply cannot be there*. In those processes I do not by any means have the objective element of the sensation, but only a form of its manifestation. We observe there other sensations, for example the motion-processes associated with that of red, which represent nothing but a metamorphosis of processes which completely dissolve into percepts. *The thing, the perceived world, is therefore nothing else than a sum total of metamorphosed percepts.* We shall never find a leap from the objectivity of the not-perceived to the subjective percept, for the percept exists as self-sustaining content.[16]

If a person is blind to red, I can never produce that quality for him conceptually. The sense-percept has a 'something' which can never pass over into the concept; it must be perceived if it is to become at all an object of knowledge. Its content is limited entirely to its 'how', to the form of its coming to appearance. We find in the concept the 'what', something that cannot be perceived.[17]

What then can be called 'subjective' in the percept? The constitution of the whole body, including sense organs and brain, which probably differs in each person. Really therefore the only thing that is subjective is the path that has to be traversed by the sensation. To the content of the sensation the concept 'subjective' is not applicable. Our organization mediates the sensation, and these mediating paths are subjective, but the sensation itself is not.[18] *

Mental pictures are not the result of physical-chemical processes but the effect of the percept-picture upon myself.

---

* For further characterization of the problem of sensation see Sections 12 and 24.

10. *The Act of Knowing*

Naive consciousness regards thinking not as something belonging to things, but as existing only in the human head. Whoever believes this need only be asked: 'What right have you to declare the world complete without thinking? Does not the world produce thinking in human heads with the same necessity that it produces the blossom on a plant? Why should the concept belong any less to the totality of the plant than the blossom?' It is quite arbitrary to regard the sum of bare percepts as a totality, while all that reveals itself through thoughtful contemplation is regarded as nothing to do with it—to regard a momentary cross-section of a process as more important than its essential nature.

It is not due to the objects that they are given to us at first without their corresponding concepts, but to our mental organization. The way I am organized has nothing to do with the things themselves. The fact is that my self-perception confines me within the sphere I perceive as my personality, but I am also the bearer of an activity which, from a higher sphere, integrates these percepts into the world process. Thinking is not individual, like our sensation or feeling—it is universal. It receives an individual stamp in each of us through its relation to our individual feelings and sensations. Although there is only one single concept 'triangle', each of us grasps it in our own individual way. This thought is opposed by a common prejudice that is very hard to overcome, but it is a fundamental requirement of philosophic thinking to do so. The concept does not become a multiplicity because it is thought by many people, for the thinking of many is in itself a unity.

In thinking we have that element which welds our separate

individuality into one whole with the cosmos. *In so far as we think, we are the all-one being that pervades everything.* This is the deeper meaning of our two-sided nature. We see coming into being in us a force complete and absolute in itself, a force which is universal, but which we learn to know not as it issues from the centre of the world, but at a point in the periphery. We explore the region outside our own being with the help of thinking, which projects into us from the universal world existence. It is this reaching out beyond our separate existence that gives rise to the desire for knowledge.

The percept is thus not something finished and self-contained, but only one side of the total reality. The other side is the concept. *The act of knowing is the synthesis of percept and concept.* Only percept and concept together constitute the whole thing. In contrast to the content of the percept, which is given from without, the content of thinking appears inwardly. The form in which this first makes its appearance we call *intuition*. Intuition is for thinking what observation is for perceiving. To explain a thing, to make it intelligible, is *to place it into the context from which it has been torn* by the peculiar character of our organization. A thing cut off from the world whole does not exist; all isolation has only subjective validity.[19]

To my perception I am, in the first instance, confined within the limits bounded by my skin. But all that is contained within this skin belongs to the world as a whole. Hence for a relation to subsist between my organization and an object outside me it is by no means necessary that something of the object should slip into me or make an impression on my mind like a signet ring on wax. The question 'How do I get information about that tree ten feet away?' is utterly misleading, springing from the view that the boundaries of my body are absolute barriers.* But the forces at work inside my body are the same as those which exist outside. Therefore, in so far as I am a part of the universal world process, I really am the things; though not of course in so far as I am a percept of myself as subject. *The percept of the tree and my 'I' belong to the same whole*, the world process producing equally the one out there and the other in here.

Our mental picture is an intuition related to a particular percept with which it was once connected, and thus *an individualized concept*. And we see how real objects can be represented subjectively by mental pictures. The full reality of a thing is given in the moment of observation through fitting together concept and percept. The concept thereby gains an individualized form that lives on in us. Reality shows itself to us as percept and concept, the subjective representative of this reality shows itself to us as mental picture. Making mental pictures gives our conceptual life an individual stamp; we think the general concepts in our own special way according to our standpoint, quite apart from our special feelings.[20]

The thing is perfectly clear. *There is only one single thought-content of the world. It requires an organ for its manifestation, and thinking is the organ which perceives it.* Dwelling in two worlds—the world of the senses pressing up from 'below', and the world of thoughts shining down from 'above'—we make ourself master of knowing by uniting the two into an undivided unity. From one side, external form beckons to us, from the other side, inner being. Thought is the essential nature of

---

* Editor's note: Wittgenstein pointed out that you have the idea that the ego is a little bird sitting inside the head, looking out through the windows of the eyes. There is no little bird.

the world, and individual human thinking is the only phenomenal form of this essential nature.[21]

Knowledge supplements and deepens what is passively perceived, by means of what our mind has lifted out of the darkness of the merely potential into the light of reality. This presupposes that sense-perception must be supplemented by the mind.[22] It is not the task of knowledge to reproduce conceptually the existent, but to produce a wholly new realm which, united with the sense world, yields full reality. Here the productivity of man's spirit finds its organic place in the world process. Cognizing only has a meaning if we see what is given by the senses as incomplete.[23] In a fact observed there is already concealed the true, the idea; we have only to remove the sheath that conceals it.[24]

We relate percepts, however, not only to concepts but also to our particular subjectivity in the form of feeling. Thinking and feeling correspond to the twofold nature of our own being: through thinking we take part in the universal cosmic process, through feeling we withdraw into the narrow confines of our own being. The former links us to the world, the latter makes us individuals. But the life of feeling is more richly saturated with reality only for my individual self. Our life is a continual oscillation between living with the universal world process and being our own individual selves. A true individuality will be the one who reaches up with his feelings to the farthest possible extent into the region of ideas. A life of feeling wholly devoid of thinking would gradually lose all connection with the world. But a human being is meant to be a whole, for whom knowledge of things goes hand in hand with the education and development of the life of feeling. Feeling is the means whereby, in the first instance, concepts gain concrete life.[25]

It cannot be too often stressed that the important thing is not that our thoughts should be in accordance with logic, but that they should *be in accordance with reality*. Logic, which is a mere description of the forms of thinking, does not alone suffice. Many people penetrate to the harmony of the world through their feelings, and when they meet the intellectual view of the world they reject with scorn its endless multiplicity.[26]

If we set ourselves questions which we cannot answer, it must be because the context of the questions is not in all respects clear and distinct. It is not the world which sets questions to us, but we who set them regarding the world. They arise through the fact that a sphere of percepts, conditioned by time, space and our subjective organization, is confronted by a sphere of concepts pointing to the totality of the universe. Our task consists in reconciling these two spheres, with both of which we are well acquainted.

The manner in which the world continuum appears to be rent asunder into subject and object thus depends on our organization as perceiving being. The object is not absolute, but merely relative in relation to this particular subject. As soon as the 'I' (the subject) fits itself back into the world continuum through thoughtful contemplation, all further questioning ceases, having been a consequence of the separation.[27]

It is part of the destiny of humanity to elevate the fundamental laws of the world, which do indeed regulate the whole of existence but which would never become existent of themselves, into the realm of realities which appear. This precisely is the essential nature of knowledge, that in it the world ground is made manifest, which in the object world can never be discovered.[28]

Since this philosophy sees the world as a single integrated whole it is formally designated as Monism.

Knowing restores the reality that our organization separates into percept and concept.

PART THREE—NATURAL PHILOSOPHY
(1885–94)

11. The Foundations of Science

We have established the relationship between experience as immediately given and the world of ideas gained by thinking. Scientific thinking must result from the step-by-step surmounting of the obscure form of reality of the former and the raising up of this into the luminous clarity of the idea. It must answer for every kind of thing: what part has it in the unitary world of ideas, in the idea-picture I form of the world? But progress in the history of science rests precisely on the fact that thinking casts up to the surface new thought-formations, linked by a thousand threads with all other possible thoughts—with one concept in one way, with another differently. Herein consists scientific method: that we show the concept of a single phenomenon in its connection with the rest of the world of ideas.

We have seen (Section 7) that each thing must necessarily require a twofold thinking effort. First the thought is established in firm outlines, and then all threads are to be determined which lead from this thought to the total thought world. Clarity in the single things and depth in the whole are the main requirements. It is obvious that the intellectual separation has only subjective existence, whereas every uniting through reason achieves the same form. We shall not therefore ask exclusively what is true and what is false, but always investigate in what way the intellectual world of a thinker separates out of the world harmony. Each person has a different field of experience, and paths to an idea may consequently differ. What matters is by no means that the single judgements and concepts agree with one another, but only that these at length guide us to swim in the channel of the idea—in which all human beings must meet if they are led by energetic thinking beyond their particular standpoint.[1]

The fundamental fallacy of established science is that it looks upon sense-perception as something inclusive, complete, and for this reason it sets itself the task simply to photograph this existence complete in itself.[2] We have seen that this is not so. (Section 10.) We must hold firmly to the fact that the total content of knowledge is given in part from outside as the sense world, in part from within as the world of ideas. All scientific activity, therefore, will consist in bringing this total content to a satisfying form.[3]

The dogma of revelation provides statements about things completely withdrawn from the horizon of our vision. Mere dogmas also are the assertions of that science which believes that we should remain at the stage of mere experience, and only observe, describe and systematically combine its modifications, without rising to the (ideal) determinants. In this case too, we do not attain to truth through insight into the phenomenon—it is forced on us from without. Today it is considered an impossibility to know anything except what the perceptible facts express. Why they speak thus and not otherwise is considered to be beyond the reach of experience and, therefore, inaccessible.

To assume the existence of a factual reason for the truth of a judgement besides the conceptual reason why we recognize it as true is nonsense. We see in the idea something completely self-contained, self-sustaining and self-upholding, which requires no added explanation from without. The Fundament of Being has been merged in the idea, has poured itself into this without any withholding, so that we have to seek for it nowhere else. In the idea, we have not an image of that which we seek in things but *that itself* for which we seek. As the parts of our world of ideas flow together in our judgements, it is the content of the idea itself which brings this about, not reasons lying outside.

It will not do to assume higher forms of existence than those belonging to the world of ideas. Only because the human being is often incapable of comprehending that the essence of the idea is a far higher, fuller essence than that of the perceived reality does he seek for still another reality. We must demand of education that it work its way upwards to that higher standpoint at which an essence that cannot be seen with eyes nor grasped with hands, but which must be conceived by reason, will also be looked upon as real.[4] To establish anything scientifically, we must limit ourselves firmly to what is given to us in consciousness. Beyond that we cannot go without finding ourselves in the unreal.[5]

Observing the processes of nature in order to employ its forces in the service of technology is entirely different from seeking with the help of these processes to see more deeply into the essential character of natural science. True science deals only with objects in the form of ideas, for its ultimate ground of existence lies in needs that derive from the spirit. The circumstance that, through our capacity for knowledge, a higher world comes to confront the world of nature of itself creates higher demands. Scientific questions are in essence something which the mind has to settle with itself. The region in which the spirit lives and moves, as in its very own, is the idea, the thought world. But modern natural science because of its whole character is unable to believe in the ideality of knowledge. This is because the idea is not accepted as the first, the most original, the most creative, but as the final product of processes in matter. But the world of ideas is more than an end product. Whereas the brain process has its source in metabolism, the reason why one thought follows another we find not in metabolism but surely in the logical thought connection. In addition to the organic necessity there holds sway in the world of thoughts a higher necessity, a necessity which the mind seeks also in the rest of the universe. The world of thoughts comes to life within us. We must however consider this thought world as underlying all that exists within the universe.[6]

Only a fallacious understanding of the concept of time has brought into existence the concept of matter. It is supposed that the world would be dissolved into mere semblance, void of being, if the fluctuating sum-total of occurrences were not conceived as resting upon something enduring in time, something unvarying. But time is not a vessel within which variations occur; it does not exist before the things and outside them. It is the sense-expression for the circumstance that the facts depend in succession on one another as to their content. Time belongs to the world of phenomena; it first appears where the essential being of a thing enters the phenomenal world. It has nothing to do with the essential being itself, which is to be grasped only in idea. Only one who cannot think the step from phenomenon to real being hypothesizes time as something preceding the facts, and then needs an existence which outlasts the changes and conceives of an indestructible matter. It is simply that one essence (itself outside time) determines another, and this process then appears as a time sequence.[7]

What then is space? Given two separate perceptible entities A and B, irrespective of what they are, our mind, wishing to relate them, says they are spatially juxtaposed—a concrete mental image. We do the same with C and D. If we now ignore the entities themselves, we can compare the two relationships AB and CD, and reach a relationship between relationships in the realm of abstraction. If thirdly we disregard what these relationships are, we have an inner relationship of space itself as ideal unity. That is why space can have only three dimensions. Absolute location, 'there', merely signifies proximity to something designated by me, like A and B. Space is thus an idea, a way to grasp the world as unity; it is not a percept.[8]

In the world of experience there are bodies of certain magnitudes and positions, there are motions and forces, and also phenomena of light, colours, heat, electricity, life, etc. As to whether these are attached to a 'matter' experience says nothing. Matter cannot be found anywhere in the world of experience. One who wishes to think it must think it up as an addition to the world of experience.[9]

Whatever does not appear within the horizon of the given does not need to be explained. It is the entity which explains a thing, appearing in our mind, that renders explanation necessary. Explanation is not a search for something unknown, but the clarification as to the mutual relationship of two known entities. There should be no talk of limits of knowledge, except in so far as we sense that some real entity is existent but at present withdrawn from our perception through some hindrance which may well be surmounted in future. Thus a legitimate hypothesis can assume only that which I should perceive if I could remove the external hindrance. It must assume that which is capable of being perceived and can be directly verified by future experience. Only hypotheses which are capable of ceasing to be hypotheses are justifiable. Hypotheses about central scientific principles have no value.[10]

If a later negative instance overthrows a law, the reason is not that the law could at first be inferred with only relative universality, but that it was not at first inferred correctly. A genuine law of nature exists as little without the facts which it determines as they exist without it.[11]

All scientific discoveries depend on the fact that the observer understands how to observe in the manner determined by the right thoughts. This he cannot do if, as scientist, he has lost faith in thinking.[12]

It is significant that the progress of science has arisen in *opposition* to what was apparent to the senses, and not in extension of it. For observation, the sun goes round the earth and the stars form a vault above; only thinking has led to speaking otherwise. It is not a question of more or better observations, but of more comprehensive ideas. The conception that from a sufficiently large number of percepts we can by induction infer the character of the underlying reality is untenable.

The task of natural science is to understand with the mind the raw data of percepts.

12. Inorganic Nature

If we are to comprehend an inorganic phenomenon such as a collision between two balls, everything present to the senses must be expressed in terms of concepts without exception, so that we can see that under the given conditions the phenomenon must occur as a matter of necessity. We can then say that concept and phenomenon coincide. The important thing here is that sense-perceptible events are determined by conditions that also belong to the sense world. Conceptual understanding is only a deduction of the sensibly real from the sensibly real; we do not need to go outside the sense world. Nothing remains obscure.

The concept here does not inhere in the occurrence itself so as to determine it, but only serves the mind as a means of comprehension; it expresses something that is sensibly real. The phenomenon in its manifoldness is thus not identical with the complex of laws that explains it, but merely points to the latter as something external to it. In a series of phenomena the concept does not reside in the individual members of the series, but in a relation of these to one another which combines the manifoldness into a whole. This relation does not come to real, concrete manifestation as such; only the members exist externally. The unity, the concept, manifests only in the intellect as the sum total. Here we have a duality, the manifold thing we perceive and the unity we think. (*Compare organic nature, Section 13.*)

Since any process whatever may here cause another, the series of events never appears anywhere as coming to an end. All is in constant reciprocal activity, without the possibility that a certain group of objects could shut themselves off from the influence of others. The inorganic chain of cause and effect has neither beginning nor end. The inorganic body is stark, to be stimulated only from without, immobile within.[13]

When the character of an event follows in transparently clear fashion directly from the nature of the factors concerned, we call it a *primal phenomenon* or fundamental fact. This is identical with a law of nature, for it expresses not only that the event happened under certain conditions, but also that it had to happen. Such a law is one of the facts, whereas induction remains external to the facts and does not penetrate to the depths.* Every law of nature is of the form: when this fact interacts with that, this phenomenon arises. All advance in knowledge depends on the perception of such primal phenomena.

However, the connection between the facts may not at first be clear. Fact A confronts us, but which of the many others are closely and which remotely related to it? In the experiment we create other combinations of facts to satisfy our need for understanding, bringing them into ideal relations suited to our minds. The mind active as intellect introduces necessity into the, at first, random phenomena but does not go beyond them.[14] In assembling the phenomena for an experiment in such a way that one fact proceeds as a matter of necessity from the other we must pass from the spatial and temporal nearest to what is nearest conceptually. An experiment is clear because we have ourselves assembled the facts.[15] It is an objective process and yet at the same time thoroughly subjective, and thus a true mediator between subject and object.

Scientific satisfaction comes only from an idea that leads to a totality complete in itself. But since in the inorganic world every event depends on another, the goal of inorganic science is a thorough understanding of the cosmos, to which every scientific endeavour is preparatory.[16]

*

Modern science, however, wrongly locates all sense qualities (sound, colour, heat, etc.) in the subject and opines that nothing corresponds with these qualities 'outside' the subject

---

* That it is why it is liable to need correction. (Ed.)

except motion-processes in matter. These, supposed to be the only thing existing in 'the kingdom of nature', naturally cannot be perceived, only inferred. But this must appear to consistent thinking as no more than a fraction of the truth. Motion, in the first place, is only a concept borrowed from the sense world, which meets us solely in connection with things possessing those other sense qualities.[17] Magnitude, form, position, motion, force, etc. are percepts in precisely the same sense as light, colours, sounds, odours, sensations of taste, heat, cold, etc. If we separate, say, the magnitude of a thing from its other characteristics and consider magnitude in itself, we are no longer dealing with a real thing, but with an abstraction of the intellect. It is the most inappropriate thing imaginable to ascribe to an abstraction taken from a sense-percept a higher degree of reality than that of a thing itself. If the modern view of nature reduces all processes of the material world to possible forms of expression in mathematics and mechanics, this is only due to the fact that the mathematical and mechanical are easy and agreeable for our thinking to handle—it inclines to the convenient.[18]

The percept 'red' cannot be derived out of motion–processes because they are an indivisible unity. They can only be separated conceptually, by the intellect. The motion-process corresponding to 'red' is an abstraction; it is itself no reality. To propose to deduce 'I see red' out of a motion-process is as absurd as proposing to deduce the real character of a salt cube out of a mathematical cube—the demand is meaningless.[19]

If a quality such as motion is transferred to non-sensible entities, such as atoms are often supposed to be, it is necessary to be clearly aware that one ascribes to a sense-perceptible attribute an imperceptible form of existence that is essentially different from the sensible. One falls into the same contradiction in seeking a real content for the completely empty concept of the atom; sense qualities have to be added back to it, even though ever so sublimated—one person attributes impenetrability, or the exertion of force, another attributes extension and the like—otherwise one remains in a complete vacuity. Therein lies the inconsistency of the theory. One thing alone is logical: if there are atoms, they are simply parts of matter with the characteristics of matter, and are not perceptible solely because their smallness renders them inaccessible to our senses. But then the possibility disappears of finding in the motion of atoms something that can be contrasted as objective with the supposedly subjective qualities of sound, colour, etc., and of finding in the connection between motion and colour anything more than exists between any two processes of the sense-world. It is clear that this theory in physics leads to a contradiction which cannot be eliminated.[20] *

If one is to avoid the contradiction of imperceptible percepts one must admit that the relationship between actual percepts can have no other mode of existence for us than that of concepts. Similarly Monism replaces imperceptible forces by idea-connections, which are gained through thinking (the laws of nature are just such conceptual connections between percepts). In the whole field of reality there is no occasion to ask for any principles of explanation other than percepts and concepts.[21]

---

* The implication is that atomic and sub-atomic phenomena are real structures of infinite complexity without any underlying 'stuff', which manifest to ordinary consciousness mathematically as concepts, but not as percepts. Only their effects ('the idea conceived as force', Section 15) can be made manifest physically. (Ed.)

The task of natural science cannot be the resolving of one kind of characteristic into another, but the finding of relations and connections among the perceptible characteristics of the sense world. The laws of mathematics and mechanics are expressions of primal phenomena, just as the laws which reduce to a formula other sense-perceptible relationships.[22]

Inorganic nature is wholly comprehended by laws existing alongside the perceptible phenomena, but not by means of partial phenomena abstracted by the intellect from the whole reality.

13. Organic Nature

In the theory of organisms, we have to fix our attention primarily upon a notable discovery of Goethe which reduces everything else to insignificance: the nature of the organism itself. What is significant in the theory of metamorphosis of plants does not lie in the discovery of the single fact that leaf, calyx, corolla, etc. are in essence identical organs, but in the magnificent thought structure of *a totality of mutually interpenetrating formative forces* which proceeds from this discovery and determines out of itself the details, the single stages in the evolution. The loftiness of this idea becomes clear only when one undertakes to rethink it. It is the concept of life. We then become aware that this thought is the very nature of the plant itself, translated into idea and living in our own mind just as in the object. One observes that an organism thus comes to life within one as something evolving, becoming, as the continuously unresting within itself.[23]

In the case of the organism, we must keep clearly in mind

most of all the fact that here the external manifestation is determined by an inner principle, that in every organ the totality is active. During his studies it became more and more clear to Goethe *that what appears in the endless multiplicity of single plant individuals is only one basic form.* His mode of observation is far more comprehensive than that of Darwin, since it embraces two aspects: firstly the entity of law manifest in the organism, which has the power and capacity to evolve in manifold external forms (species, genera); and secondly the reciprocal action between the organism and inorganic nature, and between organisms among themselves (adaptation and struggle for existence). Only the latter aspect was developed by Darwin, so that it cannot be said that Darwin's theory was the development of Goethe's basic ideas; the essential being which makes them organisms is lacking. The external conditions are merely the occasion for the inner formative forces to manifest in a special way; these latter are the constructive principle, the creative element in the plant. 'In the organ of the plant which we ordinarily designate as leaf the true Proteus lay hidden, who can conceal and reveal himself in all forms' (Goethe). The living concept that unites the forms backwards and forwards is that of alternate expansion and contraction.[24]

   To assume that the methods of inorganic science can be transferred to the study of organic phenomena ignores the fact that the organic world may not yield to such methods. So long as we negate the organism we shall never come to know it. To derive the general class of which we consider the single organism to be a particular instance, we have to conceive a basic element which is not simply determined by external conditions but which *actively determines itself* under their influence. This general organism, which includes and sustains all the particular forms, is called the *Type*. The Type is thus the idea of the organism, entirely fluid and mobile, which only reason can grasp out of the phenomenal.[25]

In the case of organisms there appear factors perceptible to the senses—form, size, colour, heat conditions of an organ—not determined by factors of a similar kind. It cannot be said that size, form, position of the roots determine the sense-perceptible characteristics of the leaves or flowers—that would be a machine. All sensible qualities appear here as a result of something *not* perceptible to the senses, but as the effects of a higher unity hovering over the sensible processes. They all exist for one another but not by reason of one another; all are determined by another entity. We must include in the concept of the phenomena elements that do not belong to the realm of the senses; we must go beyond the sense world and grasp the unity conceptually. Thus percept and concept are distinct, they no longer seem to coincide. Since the concept hovers over the percept it becomes difficult to see their connection.

Here we have to know the idea as such, for it possesses in itself something of its own that is not derived from the sense world. For this we need a power of forming judgements which can not only impart to a thought a substance taken in through the senses, but can also lay hold of that which is pure concept in itself, apart from the sense world. We call an *intuitive concept* (Section 10) one that is not taken from the sense world by abstracting but has a content flowing out of itself and only out of itself; the knowledge of such a concept may be called *intuitive knowledge*. What follows is clear: *an organism can be comprehended only through an intuitive concept.*

In the organic, the whole (the idea) determines according to its own nature every single part. This entity is the force which of itself calls itself into existence, yet is sensibly real. It has thus arrived at its sensible reality in a way wholly different from objects of the inorganic world. Yet it is clearly exposed to the influences of the sense world, like anything else. Since it is here subject not only to its own formative principles but also to outer conditions, it never appears as if in full accord with itself, never heeding only its own nature.

Here human reason enters, and forms in idea an organism heeding only its own principle, from which every accidental influence that as such has nothing to do with it falls away. This idea, the Type or archetypal organism corresponding purely with the organic aspect, is not a mere intellectual concept; it is the fully organic element without which it would not be an organism. It is indeed more real than any single actual organism, because it manifests in every organism concerned and expresses the essential being of an organism more fully, more purely than any single particular one. It is acquired by the mind in a manner essentially different from the concept of an inorganic process, and is effective in the organism as its essential being. It does not summarize the observed, but produces what is to be observed. The Type, conceived in intuitive form, explains itself. This constitutes the solution to the riddle of life.

Here the relationship of the members of a phenomenal totality comes to manifestation not only in the intellect but in the object itself. We perceive the active idea as a sensible-supersensible form through the *perceptive power of thinking*. That which explains and that which is explained are identical. The idea is thus essentially different from the concept that explains the inorganic. That is why, instead of explaining by laws of nature, we explain organic nature through the Type, where ideal and real have become a unity. The unity in idea puts forth from itself a series of organs in a temporal succession and spatial juxtaposition, and shuts itself off—unlike the inorganic—from the rest of nature in a perfectly definite way. Its states of existence are only to be comprehended by tracing the formation of successive states, proceeding out of an ideal unity. That is, *an organic entity can only be understood in its becoming*, in its evolution. It is restlessness within itself, constantly transforming itself from within outwards, transmuting, creating metamorphoses.[26]

Out of the Type, all the separate species and families are to be derived as specialized sub-types, through all the evolutionary stages, the first and equally the last. Deducing a later from an earlier is no explanation—the first in time is not the first in principle. The Type cannot be any single sensibly real entity either past or present.

The Type as *primal organism* thus corresponds to natural law as primal phenomenon. As the law controls innumerable single manifestations, so the Type manifests in innumerable different shapes. But whereas we need only recall the law and relate it to the particular facts, after apprehending the Type we must actively cause it to evolve into each particular form—the process is not one of comparison but of evolution in thought through a sequence of possibilities. We have to presuppose hypothetically determined intermediate forms through which the Type takes shape. The evolutionary method, which must replace the method of proof, is equally scientific. But the mind must work with far greater intensity, itself creating the content whilst dealing with the form. Our power of judgement must perceive in thinking and think in perceiving, so that intuition replaces judgement through proof. Intuition is the actual being—within the world process with our thinking.

We do not think 'about' organic nature, but thinking enters into direct connection with the reality.[27]

Living organisms can only be understood by living ideas, in which the mind works intuitively and creatively in response to hereditary and environmental factors.

14. Human Nature

The human being, to the extent that he is a creature of nature, is to be understood also according to the laws applicable to the action of nature. But as a cognizing or truly ethical being he steps outside the realities of nature. His life-course is to free himself from all natural laws and become his own law-giver.[28]

Animal life severs itself from the body and uses it as a tool. An animal's form and hence its manner of life is determined from within, but its life also exists outside the form as its controlling power and has a centre which every organ serves. Each organ system can attain a certain degree of development, hence the possibility of differentiation according to adaptation.[29]

In the developed form of the human being Goethe seeks to rediscover the animal forms, only that in the animal the organs serving primarily animal functions come into the foreground, constituting as it were the point towards which the entire formation is directed and which it serves, whereas the human form develops specially those organs which serve the function of the mind. What hovered before him as the animal organism is not this or that sensibly real entity, but again an entity in idea.

The human structure as a totality reaches such perfection as to be capable of being the bearer of a free spiritual being. All the organs and organ systems develop in such a way that each leaves to the others space enough for its free development; each one retires within the limits which appear needful in order that all the others may in like measure assert themselves. Thus arises a harmonious working together, the human uniting in himself the perfections of all other creatures. Moreover in Goethe's own mind, no single branch of human endeavour pressed forward to the neglect of all others, but the totality of human existence always hovered in the background while he was dealing with a single field.[30]

Our instincts, urges and passions establish no more than that we belong to the general human species; it is the fact that something of the idea world comes to expression in a particular way that establishes individuality. One cannot say of the action of a criminal that it proceeds from the idea within him, from what is individual; indeed it characteristically springs from the non-ideal elements, from what is most general in him.[31]

If the world were populated merely by sentient creatures its essential (ideal) content would remain forever hidden. Laws would of course control the world process, but they would never become manifest. If that is to occur there must be a being who can perceive not only the sense-reality but also the conformity to law itself. It is here perfectly clear that our mind must be conceived as an organ that perceives the thoughts.[32]

Human feeling is exactly the same on the subjective side as the percept is on the objective. Hence it must be the guarantee of the reality of our own personality. Yet it is an incomplete reality, lacking the concept or idea. Only gradually does the concept of self emerge from within the dim feeling of our existence.[33]

Self-observation shows that the ego not only affirms its own existence, but strives in its many-sided development to comprehend by thinking the whole world content, building up its world picture by the synthesis of the given with concepts. Were it not for this activity, the world of objects would not exist in consciousness. If we watch it in its constructive activity, we understand the foundation of the finished world picture.[34]

The something more which we seek in things over and above what is immediately given splits our whole being into two parts: I and world. We erect this barrier between ourselves and the world as soon as consciousness first dawns in us. Despite this, we never cease to feel that we belong to the world, that there is a connecting link between it and us, and that we are within and not outside the universe. Religion, art, science—the whole of our spiritual striving seeks to bridge this gap. We have ourselves created this threshold, and must find within ourselves the part of nature which as more than 'I' will restore the missing link.[35] Human consciousness thus has to do with spiritual content itself. Knowledge here plays a different role; it is an interpretation of the human being to himself. The destiny of the person is to achieve, even as ideal entity, actual self-sustaining existence.[36]

Natural law, type and concept are the three forms in which ideas manifest. Natural law is abstract, existing above the sense-perceptible multifariousness, and dominates in inorganic science where idea and reality fall completely apart. In organic nature the type unites the two, the spiritual becomes an operative being; not present as such, but present in a perceptible way. In human consciousness, the concept itself is perceptible—percept and idea coincide. For this reason the ideal essential centres of existence of the lower stages of nature also come to manifestation. Through human consciousness, what at lower stages merely is but does not become manifest may now become reality in manifestation.[37]

The genuine, truest form of nature comes to manifestation in the human mind, whereas for a mere sense-being only nature's external aspect would exist. Knowledge plays here a role of world significance—it is the conclusion of the work of creation.[38]

The onesidedness of animals is in humanity harmonized to enable a higher element to enter.

PART FOUR—MORAL PHILOSOPHY
(1885–94)

15. Ethics

The spiritual or cultural sciences require an essentially different attitude of mind from the natural sciences. Here consciousness has to do with spiritual content, with the individual human spirit and the creations of culture—literature, science, art. The spiritual is grasped by the spirit. Reality here possesses in itself the ideal, conformity to law, which elsewhere appears first in mental conception. The human being should himself fix the purpose, the goal of his existence, his activity. He must know the spiritual world in order to take his share in it. This the cultural sciences—psychology, the science of peoples, the science of history—have to achieve.[1]

A human personality has only those traits, characteristics and capacities which it ascribes to itself through insight into its own being. This determines the method of research in the field of human nature: neither proof nor evolution of the Type, but the immersion of the mind in its own activity, namely, *self-apprehension.* We release the single mind from its fortuitous limitations and accessory traits, and rise to consider the human individual as such. Whereas the Type confronts its single forms, the general is here active immediately in the individual, though in various ways; it is itself determined by the particular.

The *human spirit* has only one form, but in one case certain objects move the feelings, in another the ideal inspires an action. It is not a specialized form of the human spirit but always the entire and complete human being with which we have to deal. We must discover how the human spirit behaves in general, not how it has behaved in this or that situation. The spiritual human being is not *one* formation of its idea, but *the* formation of it. *In perceiving the single forms we recognize the primal form itself.* We have to separate this human spirit from its manifestations and turn to the spirit itself as the producer of these. Psychologists usually limit themselves to the manifestations and forget the spirit. In all manifestations of the human spirit—thinking, feeling and willing—the important thing is to recognize these in their essential nature as expressions of the *personality*.[2]

Our theory of knowledge recognizes no other basis for truths than the thought content residing within them. When therefore a moral ideal comes into existence, it is the inner power lying in its content which governs our conduct. The ideal, by virtue of its content, is active within us, it directs us. The impulse towards conduct lies not outside us but within us. The will is sovereign; it performs only what lies as thought-content in the personality. A human being is not behaving in accordance with the purposes of the Guiding Power of the world when he investigates one or another of His commandments, but when he behaves according to his own insight; for in him the Guiding Power of the world manifests Himself. To act morally is not the fulfilment of duty, but the expression of our wholly free nature. We act, not because we ought, but because we will, according to our insight.[3]

In cognition we make manifest the ideas within reality, the hidden producing agent; in action we transform this thought world into a reality, to the extent that it is not so already. Our action appears as a continuation of the sort of activity nature carries out as a direct outflow of the World Fundament. Here the idea dwells within the one who acts, and a perfect human action is the result of our purposes and only these. When one product of nature acts on another, the effect leads us to the concept of force, where the idea connecting the objects appears as causative. *Will is thus the idea conceived as force.* It cannot be said that will must be added to the concept. If we wish to comprehend will, we arrive at the thought world engaged in action. Will without idea would be nothing. The entity of law which determines a phenomenon enters itself into the action. A person's deed is understood when we know his intention.[4]

Thus our conduct is determined by our moral ideals, the ideas we have of our tasks in life; and as part of the world process, this is subject to universal laws. Every event has its external sequence in time and space, and its internal conformity to law. *It is knowledge of this conformity to law* which makes our conduct truly ours, for it is then the very substance of our ego. The law then rules *in* us, not over us. To gain knowledge of the laws of one's own conduct is thus to become conscious of freedom. Only in so far as our life falls into this realm can it be called moral. To transform unfree into free actions is the task of self-development for the individual and for the whole human race. The most important problem for thinking is to conceive the human being as a personality grounded on itself and free.[5]

Moral intuitions and imaginations (Section 16) can only become objects of knowledge after they have been produced by an individual in unique circumstances. The study of them, the subject matter of ethics, is the natural science of morality, and like all other sciences concerns what already is, not what should be.[6] General laws of ethics, norms supposed to be valid for all, prove utterly worthless. Not everything is equally worthy of being carried out by everyone, but one thing for this person and another for that, according as each one feels the call to do a certain thing. Ethics is supposed to give a detailed answer to the question 'What is good?' But such a science is impossible. There are no general laws as to what should be done or not done.[7]

Nevertheless moral laws are important for those who are as yet unable to grasp moral intuitions for themselves, but are able to receive them as ideas arising from generalizations of individual intuitions in the past. It is on the path towards the goal of freedom that these play a legitimate part. Nature makes of human beings merely natural beings; society makes them law-abiding beings; only individuals can make of themselves free beings.[8]

On this view many problems of ethics fall away. Abstract discussions of optimism and pessimism, for example, dissolve into the question whether our desire for a goal is greater than the hindering effect of the pain involved. If we strive for sublimely great ideals, it is because they are the content of our being, and their realization brings a joy compared with which the gratification of commonplace desires is trivial.[9]

The spirit is the universal source for all moral deeds; but those who cannot rise to it need moral laws from those who can.

16. The Free Spirit

Is a person in his thinking and acting spiritually free, or is he compelled by the iron necessities of natural law or of logic? Is one entitled to claim for oneself freedom of will, and if so, under what circumstances? For it is surely obvious that much of what we do is instinctive or impulsive. But what about deliberate actions, where we know why we are acting? The question is not whether we can carry out decisions once made, but how decisions come about within us. Are there any motives except such as compel us with absolute necessity?[10]

Understanding of this problem depends on recognizing the conclusion already reached (Section 10), that thinking derives from an intuition of spiritual content, and not from our psycho-physical organization. We do not say that footprints in the soil are formed by the ground below; neither should we say that thinking is formed by traces in the physical brain, but rather that it produces those traces. If we would grasp most immediately the essential nature of spirit, we need only look at the self-sustaining activity of thinking, where concept and percept—which must otherwise appear apart—coincide. If we fail to see this fact, we shall only regard concepts as shadowy copies of the percepts that we take for reality. When we observe our thinking we live during this observation directly within a self-sustaining spiritual essence brought into our consciousness through intuition. Intuition is the conscious experience—in pure spirit—of a purely spiritual content.

Only if we have worked our way through to recognizing this can we see that the psycho-physical organization can have no effect on *the essential nature* of thinking. For this organization contributes nothing to the essential nature, but recedes whenever the activity of thinking appears, suspends its activity and yields ground. And on the ground left empty thinking appears. The essence that is active in thinking first represses the activity of the organism, and then steps into its place. The repression is more particularly a consequence of that part of the activity which prepares its manifestation. (Section 24.)

Just as knowledge depends on the union of concept and

percept, so an act of will depends on the coming together of a conceptual factor as motive and the will factor of the bodily organism as driving force. The *motive or intention* is the momentary determining cause, and may be a pure concept or a concept with a definite relation to a percept (i.e. a mental picture). But whether the motive is adopted or not (whether the idea of a walk appeals) depends on a more permanent factor in the individual, the *disposition of character or driving force* determined especially by previous mental pictures and feelings. Moreover both motives and driving force are of various levels.

At the first level of individual life, in which sense-perception leads immediately to action, the driving force involved in satisfying purely animal needs may be called 'instinct', whilst in conventional intercourse it becomes 'tact'. At a second level, feelings like pity, shame, pride, loyalty, love or duty accompany the sensations and lead to action. At a third level, reflection or practical experience in the past may give rise to mental pictures that are put straight into action. The highest level is that of conceptual intuition, pure thinking, without regard to any direct perceptual content.

Similarly the lowest level of motive is the concrete mental picture of one's own pleasure or welfare (pure egoism), or the welfare of another (altruism). Secondly there are the moral principles dictated by some moral authority, either external (parent, custom, law, Church) or internal (revelation, conscience). Thirdly one may try to understand the reason for moral maxims, and act on the mental picture one forms of the best way to promote the greatest good of mankind, or the progress of civilization, and so on. Lastly, one may seek the pure conceptual intuition appropriate to the immediate situation.

Thus at the highest level both driving force and motive coincide in *pure thinking* or conceptual intuition; the action is determined purely and simply by its own ideal content. Whoever lacks the capacity to experience for himself the particular moral principle for each single situation will never achieve truly individual willing. In so far as this intuitive content of effective ideas applies to action, it constitutes the moral content of the individual.

Whilst I am acting I am influenced by a moral maxim in so far as it lives within me intuitively; it is bound up with my love for the objective I want to realize. If someone acts only because he accepts certain moral standards, he merely carries out orders. Inject some stimulus into his mind, and the clockwork of his moral principles brings about an action which is Christian, or humane, or seemingly unselfish. *Only when I follow my love for my objective is it I myself who act.* I acknowledge no external principle for my action, because I have found in myself the ground for it, namely, my love of the action. My action will be 'good' if my intuition, steeped in love, finds its right place within the intuitively experienced world continuum; it will be 'bad' if this is not the case. I feel no compulsion, neither of nature which guides me by instincts nor of moral commandments, but I will, simply to carry out what lies within me. I am free in so far as I can obey myself in every moment of my life.[11]

Thus a free spirit acts according to *moral intuitions* selected by thinking from the totality of the world of ideas. He has purely ideal reasons which lead him to select from the sum of his concepts just one in particular and translate it into action. He makes a completely original decision. But his action will have to belong to perceptible reality, the concept will have to realize itself in a specific occurrence. As a concept, however, it cannot contain this event, but only refer to it in the way a concept in general relates to a percept. Now the link between concept and percept is the mental picture. For the unfree spirit, motives are present from the outset in the form of mental pictures; he acts as he has seen it done or been told to do. For the free spirit, the transformation of the concept into mental picture is always necessary, and this is done chiefly by means of the imagination or fantasy. Therefore what the free spirit needs in order to implement his ideas so that they are effective is moral imagination, moral fantasy. Therefore only those with *moral imagination* are morally productive.

In order to transform a definite perceptual situation in accordance with a moral mental picture, one must have grasped the way it has hitherto worked and discover the procedure by which to change it. This depends on knowledge of the particular phenomena concerned, which can be learned like any other knowledge. Moral action thus presupposes, in addition to having moral intuition and moral imagination, also the ability to transform the world of percepts without violating the natural laws by which these are connected. This ability is *moral technique*. People are usually better at finding concepts for the existing world than evolving imaginations of the future, whilst those with moral imagination may lack technique, and so on.

To be free means to be able of one's own accord to determine by moral imagination those mental pictures (motives) which underlie one's action. Freedom is impossible if anything other than myself (e.g. mechanical process or merely inferred extra-mundane God) determines my moral ideas. In other words, I am free only when I myself produce these mental pictures.[12]

The view outlined here is called *ethical individualism*. It may well be true that this concept of freedom is rarely found. But in all the welter of customs, legal codes, religious observances and so forth there arise those who establish themselves as free spirits. Who can say he is truly free in all his actions? Yet in each of us there dwells a deeper being in which the free man finds expression. An individual's true concept of moral being (free spirit) is not objectively united from the start with the percept 'human being', as it is for everything else. We must unite our concept with the percept by our own activity, and this we can only do if we have found the concept of the free spirit, that is, the concept of our own self.[13]

True freedom is the highest objective of mankind.

17. Social Aspects

Political science and ethnology have to show what form the organism of the state must assume if it is to express the individuality of a people. The constitution is its individual character brought into form of law. Whoever would indicate beforehand the direction in which a definite activity of a people has to move must not impose anything from without, but simply express what lies unconscious in the character of the people.[14]

As a human being you belong not only to yourself—you belong as a member to two higher totalities. First, you are a member of your people, with whom you are united through common moral customs, a common cultural life, a language, and a common view of things. Secondly you are a citizen of history, a single member in the great historical process of humanity's evolution. Through this your free action appears to be impaired. But by means of your capacity for knowledge you can penetrate into the character of your individual people, and it becomes clear whither your fellow citizens are steering. That by which you seem to be determined you can surmount and take into yourself as a fully known concept; it then becomes individual and takes on completely the personal character that is possessed by actions performed in freedom. So it is likewise concerning historical evolution; we can elevate ourselves to knowledge of the leading ideas, the moral forces, which there hold sway. In short, we must work our way upwards, in order that we may not be guided but may guide ourselves. To this end, it is most important of all that we understand our own time. The spiritual is grasped by the spirit, and the human being must know the world of the mind and determine his participation in it accordingly.

Legal statutes are nothing but the outflow of individual intuitions imparted to a whole people. A universal natural law that would be valid for all human beings at all times is non-existent. Conceptions of rights and of ethics come and go with peoples—indeed with individuals. Always the individuality is the determining factor. There can be no science of human action itself, for it is undetermined, free, creative. Jurisprudence is not a science, but a collection of notes on those practices in the sphere of rights that belong to an individual people.

Every personality represents a spiritual potency, a sum total of forces which search for the possibility of action. Therefore every person must find the place where their work may be articulated in the most fruitful way into the organism of their people; it must not be left to chance. The state constitution has properly no other goal than to ensure that everyone shall find his appropriate place. The state is the form in which the organism of the people expresses itself.[15] General laws of history are such only in so far as they were set up by historical personalities as goals or ideals. The particular establishes the law, and is our sole interest.[16]

Anyone who believes that a social community is possible only if everyone is united by a communally fixed set of moral laws need only reflect that the world of ideas working in me is no other than the one working in themselves. If we both really conceive out of the idea and do not obey any external influences (physical or spiritual) then we cannot but meet in a common intent. A moral misunderstanding, a clash, is impossible between those who are morally free. Clashes arise through following one's natural instincts or differing commands of duty. Indeed, it is only because human beings are one in spirit that they can live out their lives side by side. The free person does not demand agreement from others, but expects to find it because it is inherent in human nature. To live in love towards our actions, and to let live in the understanding of the other person's will is the fundamental maxim of those who are free.

The free spirit seldom needs to go beyond the laws of his state, and certainly never needs to place himself in real opposition to them when those laws—just like all other objective laws of morality—have had their origin in the intuition of free spirits. The only person who feels unfree is the one who forgets this origin and turns them into extra-human commandments or into a commanding voice within himself. Those who do not overlook this origin yet believe they have better intuitions will try to put them in place of the existing ones; if they find them justified, they will treat them as their own.

State and society exist only as a necessary consequence of

the life of individuals, for the individual would become stunted by an isolated existence outside human society. The social order arises so that it may in turn react favourably upon the individual.[17] What appears as the common goal of a group of people is only the result of the separate acts of will of its individual members, and in fact usually of a few outstanding ones who, as their authorities, are followed by the others.[18]

The view that the human being is destined to become a free individuality seems to be contested by the fact that we appear as a member of a naturally given totality (race, people, nation, family, sex) and also work within a totality (state, Church and so on), and bear general characteristics of the group. Consequently the physiognomy and conduct of individuals do have something generic about them. People make themselves free however from the group and develop qualities and activities of their own, using as a foundation the characteristics given by nature. How an individual has to think cannot possibly be deduced from any kind of generic concept.

If we would understand a single individual we must find our way to their own particular being, and in this sense every single human being is a separate problem. We must cease to call to our aid any concepts at all of our own making, and take over into our own spirit in their pure form those concepts by which they determine themselves.[19]

To be free within society we need to make the ideas of our people and of history our own.

18. Aesthetics

We have seen that knowledge is the product of the activity of the human mind as idea. In true art too we elevate ourself from the product to the reality which produces, from created to creation, from chance to necessity; our mind rises from the particular to the fountainhead in which innumerable potentialities are contained. An object of the external world is so transformed as to appear as a representative of the all-inclusive. The infinite, which science seeks in the finite and endeavours to represent as idea, is stamped by art on material existence. Hence the true artist must create out of the fountainhead of existence. The material substance remains, except that its non-essentials must be completely subdued by the artistic treatment; the object must be freed from accidentals, and transferred entirely into the sphere of the inevitable. The 'what' must be surmounted by the 'how'. Thus real art surmounts the sense-perceptible by implanting the spirit into it. Whereas science sees the idea through the sensible, art sees it in the sensible.[20]

Whereas scientists immerse themselves in the depths of reality in order to be able to express its impelling forces in the form of thoughts, artists seek by imagination to embody the same impelling forces in their material. Not what nature has created but according to what principles it has created is the important question. Thus art rests upon cognition. Cognition has the task of recreating in thought the order according to which the world is put together; genuine art has the task of forming in single objects the idea of this order of the world totality. Everything that is attainable by artists of the nature of this world law-conformity is put into their work. Thus this becomes manifest as a world in miniature. True art flows from the primal fountainhead of existence; it tells of the entity of law learned from the World Spirit, and becomes the interpreter of world mysteries.[21] We understand a work of art when we know the idea embodied in it.[22]

Humanity needs this new kingdom, in which the particular is endowed with the character of the universal and necessary, and this has first to be created. The artist has to raise the material into the sphere of the divine. Genuine beauty is a phenomenon in the form of the idea, physical reality in a cloak that is divine. It is however a real semblance, when the physical and individual, arrayed in the imperishable raiment of eternity, appears with the character of the idea; for reality falls short of this.[23]

In his study of colour, Goethe remained in the realm of phenomena, in their becoming; he then comes to their sensible moral effects, which Newton does not.[24] What spiritual reality underlies colour percepts? Light (as distinct from sunlight) is a purely spiritual entity. It is modified by opaque lightlessness, active darkness. It is not that light and darkness are actually contained in colour—only the mind can analyse the sense-perceptible fact into two spiritual entities. One must look on light and darkness as such entities, which are unknown to physics. It is a different world view.[25]

All real philosophers have been artists in the realm of culture; human ideas are their material, and scientific method their technique. Such ideas can become powerful forces in life.[26]

True art is the purest expression of the idea.

19. Metaphysics

The total fundamental essence of Being has poured itself out into the world. It is manifest in thought in its most complete form, just as it is, and of itself. If thinking forms a combination, if a judgement occurs, it is the content of the World Fundament itself, poured out into thought, which is thus united in us. Postulates are not given to us about a yonder-side World Fundament, but in its very substance this has flowed into thought. Nothing need be conceded to revelation for which thought does not contain objective reasons. The essential nature of a thing comes to light only when it is brought into relation to a human being, for only then does its essential being become manifest. The world is not only known to us as it appears, but it appears as it is, although only to thinking contemplation. The form of reality which we delineate in our knowledge is its final true form.[27] A thing that could not be comprised within thought would be a no-thing. Our thought is bound to the hither-side, and knows nothing of a yonder-side.[28]

The elevation of the human being is enhanced through the fact that whatever we create is cruelly destroyed; for we must ever build and create anew, and it is in action that our happiness lies, in what we ourselves achieve. Seeking ourselves for truth—this alone is worthy of mankind. Once this is understood through and through, people will no longer desire that God reveal Himself to them or bestow blessings on them. They will desire to attain knowledge and happiness through their own efforts. The loftiest idea of God remains the assumption that after creating mankind He withdrew from the world and left us wholly to ourselves.*

Thinking as a capacity of perception implies the existence of entities beyond sense-perceptible reality, namely, ideas. As thinking takes possession of the idea it merges into the pri-

---

* We are today able to accept or reject the impulses brought by Christ Jesus—or those of evil. (Ed.)

mordial foundation of the world; that which works without
enters into the human spirit. We become one with objective
reality at its highest potency. *Becoming aware of the idea
within reality is the true communion of mankind.*[29]

In the idea we recognize that out of which we must derive
everything else, the principle of things. Hence what the
philosophers call the Absolute, the Eternal Being, the World
Fundament, what the religions call God, we call the idea. All
must become part of the great whole which the idea encom-
passes; but the idea does not require that one go beyond it. In
taking possession of the idea, we attain to the core of the
world. Thinking is not the creator of the idea-content of the
world, but the organ of perception. If only we can press
forward all the way to the world of ideas, we can be sure that
we possess at last a world common to all human beings, even
though we may grasp it in a very one-sided way.

What is gained in the individual sciences is the objective
foundation of world existence. Now for the first time we
know that we are most directly linked with this central core,
that the World Spirit manifests in us, that this Spirit dwells in
us. We see in ourself one who is to complete the world process. Thus the theory of knowledge is likewise the teaching of
the significance and destiny of humanity.[30]

Since the World Fundament comes to light in its own form
in thinking, we cannot but recognize a human action as the
undetermined action of that primal fundament itself. The
Lord of the World has surrendered His power and imparted
to mankind the task: continue to work. We find in nature the
indication of an intention, it becomes our spiritual possession, and we proceed to carry out that intention. This is a
true philosophy of freedom.[31]

Metaphysics is thus replaced by contemplation, synthesizing, deducing primal phenomena.[32] A sound human thinking holds to this world, and does not concern itself with any other. At the same time, however, it spiritualizes this world.[33]

Monism denies all justification to metaphysics, which merely draws inferences, and consequently also to impulses of action which are derived from so-called 'Beings-in-themselves'. It cannot recognize any unconscious compulsion hidden behind percept and concept. The moral laws which the metaphysician regards as issuing from a higher power are for adherents of Monism merely human thoughts. For them the moral world order is neither the imprint of a mechanical natural order nor of an extra-human world order, but through and through the free creation of human beings. Monism does not see, behind human actions, the purposes of a supreme directorate, foreign to us and determining us according to its will, but rather that we each pursue our own particular human ends. For the world of ideas comes to expression only in individuals. Just as beings of a different order will understand knowledge to mean something very different from what it means to us, so will they have a different morality. Morality is a specifically human quality, and spiritual freedom the human way of being moral.[34]

Philosophy leads only to the outpoured World Fundament.

20. The Consequence of Monism

Monism, the uniform explanation of the world, derives what it needs from human experience, and looks for the sources of action in the part of human nature accessible to self-knowledge, more particularly in moral imagination. The unity that thoughtful observation—which we can experience—brings to the manifold multiplicity of percepts is the same unity through which our need for knowledge seeks entry into the physical and spiritual regions of the world.

The single individual is not actually cut off from the universe but is part of it, and between this part and the totality of the cosmos there exists a real connection which is broken only for our perception. *All separate existence turns out to be mere illusion due to perceiving.* Thinking destroys this illusion, and integrates our individual existence into the life of the cosmos. We can find our full and complete existence in the totality of the universe only through the experience of intuitive thinking. Thinking gives us reality in its true form as a self-contained unity.

The content of a concept is not subjective, but is the part of reality that cannot be reached by perceiving. If someone cannot see this, he is thinking only of the abstract form he holds in his own mind. An abstract concept by itself has as little reality as a percept by itself. Our mental organization tears the reality apart into these two factors; only the reunion of the two, the percept fitting systematically into the universe, constitutes full reality. In so far as we find the ideas that belong to the percept, we are living in reality, and have no need to look beyond this for a higher reality that can never be experienced.

One human individual regards another as akin because the same world content expresses itself in both—thinking leads all perceiving subjects to the same ideal unity. As soon as we look at the ideas within ourselves, encompassing all that is separate, we see the absolute reality living and shining forth. We find the divine life, common to all, in reality itself. But everyone embraces in his thinking only a part of the total world of ideas, and to that extent individuals differ in the actual content of their thinking. But all these contents are within a self-contained whole. Hence every man, in his thinking, lays hold of the universal primordial Being, which pervades all men. To live in reality, filled with the content of thought, is at the same time to live in God.

A world beyond which is merely inferred and cannot be experienced arises from a misconception of the nature of thinking. That is why no speculation has ever brought to light any content that was not borrowed from the reality given to us. The truth is that the human spirit never transcends the reality in which we live, nor has it any need to do so. All attempts to transcend the world are purely illusory, and principles transferred into the Beyond do not explain the world any better than those which remain within it. A primordial Being for which we invent a content is an impossible assumption for any thinking that understands itself.

Just as little can the aims of our action be derived from an extra-human Beyond. We pursue our individual purposes given by our moral imagination. It is not commandments injected from Beyond that live in our actions, but our intuitions belonging to this world. We recognize no World Dictator directing our actions, but are thrown back on ourselves. If we are to go beyond satisfying our natural instincts, we must seek the grounds in our own moral imagination or let ourselves be determined by the moral imaginations of others. If an idea is to become action, a person must first *want* it; we are the ultimate determinants of our own actions. We are free.[35]

Monism is the philosophical expression of human freedom.

PART FIVE—BIOGRAPHICAL

21. Weimar (1889–95)

Before leaving Vienna, Steiner completed a third volume for the Kürschner edition of Goethe's works, published in 1891. He also came to terms with mysticism, which he found strengthened the inner life of feeling but effaced true experience of the spiritual world.[1] About that time he took Goethe's tale of the Green Snake and the Beautiful Lily as important material for meditation. And he also submitted his dissertation for Ph.D., adapted from his *Theory of Knowledge* and published as *Truth and Science* (1892), to a specialist on Plato's relationship to Christianity. On moving his mood was thus tinged with Platonism.[2]

He outlines in his Autobiography his thinking at this turning point, summarized very briefly as follows: 'The sense world is no complete reality. Finding the spirit in the sense world is not a question of logical inferences or of the extension of sense-perception, but something that comes to pass when we continue our evolution to the experience of sense-free thinking. When we seek true reality by sinking into the inner life, sense-free thinking places the soul within the spiritual being of the world. When it then meets sense-perception, it rediscovers the spiritual content in the perceptual world, and that is "knowing". We are actually inside the being of things. Our spiritual being acts only through moral intuitions, which are experienced in the world of pure spirit but recognized merely as sense-free thoughts.'[3]

In the Goethe archives at Weimar he met what he called

'mummies of classicism and pedantic philology'. But he describes himself as living among the Archangel Michael and his opponents, with an intense and momentous experience of the actual spiritual world.[4] Especially in this last decade of the nineteenth century, only a thin veil concealed the great battle of Michael and everything connected with him. And it was by no means rarely that Steiner caught a glimpse through the veil.[5]

From spiritland Steiner 'visited' (as he put it) the physical world, having to look at things many times in order to grasp them. He also 'visited' the world conceptions of others, entering deeply into the few friendships brought by destiny, and forming pictures of them in creative fantasy.[6] In conversations with painters and musicians his artistic experiences developed, yet he held to his own views. He came into contact with such people as Dr Breuer, Hermann Grimm and Haeckel, and heard Mahler and Richard Strauss perform. But none of those he met could enter into his own world view, so that his inner loneliness was still intense.

It was between the ages of 30 and 33 that he finally brought to expression his *Philosophy of Freedom* (1894). 'I felt I was setting down the thoughts that the spiritual world had given me up to my 30th year; what had come from the outer world merely provided the stimulus.' It was especially the deep abyss which current thinking had created between nature and the moral-spiritual world that struck him. He perceived in the spiritual facts and beings of the world above nature a veritable reality. His first objective was to show that the sense-world is in reality spiritual, that no unknown lies behind the sense world, but that ideas themselves exist there. His second objective was to characterize the moral world as spirit shining into the soul's experience, enabling it to arrive at the moral world in freedom. He thereby brought to a conclusion his long struggle with Kantianism and scientific thinking based on metaphysical entities.[7]

He now came across Nietzsche's works, and in 1895 published *Nietzsche as Adversary of his Age*. He saw Nietzsche in his illness, and could admire and sympathize with his spiritual struggle based on mythology. But he was shocked at what he found when asked to arrange his library, and would not edit his works.[8]

Through a strange destiny with two men he had never met but knew through their families, he saw how materialistic thoughts need not lead away from spiritual perception nor after death alienate a person from the spiritual world, whereas materialistic willing does so.[9]

During his last year in Weimar a profound revolution began in his mind. Now he felt that the physical sense world itself has something which it alone can reveal, about which spiritual perception has nothing to say. 'In observing the physical we go right out of ourselves, and thus come with intensified capacity back into the spirit. The whole world except man is a riddle, but thought only brings the soul towards the solution. Man himself is in reality the solution, but only so much as he understands of himself.' (Section 28.) This was a living inspiration for what Steiner called 'knowledge by way of reality', where one provides the stage on which beings and events of the world for the first time partly experience their own existence. Haeckel also surrendered to physical vision, there is no better basis for scientific esotericism; but his ideas were limited by old religious politics.

Secondly his meditation, hitherto undertaken because he knew its value, now became a necessity of life. Experience through ideas, the basis of his *Philosophy*, became an intimate living communion with the world. And through release from the body as though it were not there, the consciousness of an 'inner spiritual man' evolved, who can live, perceive and move in the spiritual world. Thirdly, as knowledge through ideas in a way retired, the element of will increasingly took its place (also in spiritual knowledge) and thinking took more from willing. (Section 27.) Thus the capacity of the whole of the human being to grow into every form of being had to be recognized, fully conscious that one stands within the cosmos. Talk of an 'unknown spirit' in some sort of beyond is then specially harmful. If however one relates to the sense world so that one thing explains another, one may extend this to the spiritual.[10]

Fourthly, 'My ethical individualism also changed from a conceptual element to something that laid hold on the entire man. I found that the divine spiritual forces which are the inner soul of our will have no way of access from the outer world to the inner man. The moral proceeds out of the soul, it must exist in its entirely individual being. The moral world order stood out in ever clearer light as the one realization on earth of such ordered systems of action as are found in spiritual regions above. One event can only be explained by another event, and the human being himself becomes the outer word for the world he perceives. That which holds sway in the world is the Logos, Wisdom, the Word; and the human being becomes the Word. The soul lives in the Logos, but how does the external world live in the Logos? That was the basic question of my *Philosophy*.'[11]

22. Berlin (1896–1902)

After completing the last volume of the Kürschner edition, writing *Goethe's World Conception* (1897)—which he did not permit to be coloured by own views—and editing the works of Schopenhauer, fate placed Steiner in an activity that no longer corresponded with his inner life.[12] As part of his experience of the question 'Must one remain speechless?' he seized an opportunity to edit the *Magazin fur Literatur* in Berlin, but a co-editor was appointed through which unsurmountable difficulties arose. This he accepted as his destiny. Associated with it was a Literary Society (mainly young) and a Dramatic Society, where he gave introductory talks, acted as stage manager, and wrote the reviews (depicting the germ in the author's mind). None of this gave inner satisfaction, though he met people of many kinds.[13] The *Magazin* proved a constant source of anxiety, because its small circulation afforded him only the bare necessities of material existence; and he suffered from the utter misery of living alone in a strange city. 'The Angels pressing towards Ahriman* grew strong.'[14]

At the same time he encountered a severe test in that the 'beyond' teaching of the churches referred to a world of spirit unattainable by human beings, whereas he himself had experienced the spiritual world since his youth, and had expressed in his *Philosophy* a morality in which lived the divine. This was for him no mere matter of thought, but he had to save his spiritual perception in real inner battles with actual spiritual beings for whom it is an absolute truth that the world must be a machine; it was a fierce struggle with a Being who is error. His soul was here torn into a surging abyss.[15] He felt in 1898 that his ethical individualism, a pure human inner experience, had to be changed to something more exoteric and external, such as a philosophy of politics;

---

* Satan, the power of destruction and materialism.

and what he said about social matters became all too radical.[16] He regarded this period as his most intense spiritual test; but a spiritual pupil has to experience this, because from it comes a great access to forces later needed to work outwards from the spirit.[17]

The year 1899 was in fact the end of Kali Yuga, the oriental Dark Age of 5000 years, and the beginning of the new Age of Light. At this difficult time he was invited to lecture at the Berlin Workers School, initially on history and public speaking, and later on natural science. He agreed on condition that he gave only his own views, and had to find his way into the proletariat mind, where souls that craved knowledge slumbered and dreamed whilst a kind of mass soul laid hold on them with materialism. He had much success for several years, until the Marxist leaders drove him out.[18] Meanwhile the mother of the boys he had tutored, now a widow, came to Berlin and offered him the best of care, which led to their civil marriage but subsequent separation.[19]

He wrote his first esoteric article for the *Magazin,* on Goethe's tale of the Green Snake, and then resigned in order to lecture from his research. His 'basic anthroposophical lecture' to the Giordano Bruno Union was debated on the streets till 3.00 a.m.! To The Coming Ones he gave 27 lectures on 'Anthroposophia'. And in a small branch of the Theosophical Society he could regularly speak entirely esoterically, though the Society's literature was still either unknown or uncongenial to him.[20]

About the turn of the century, the germ of the real content of Christianity and its actual evolution unfolded for him more and more directly out of the spiritual world. This was an inner phenomenon in which the meaning of Earth evolution became clear. 'The evolution of my soul rested on the fact that

I stood before the Mystery of Golgotha in most inward, most earnest joy of knowledge.'[21] 'Not I, but Christ in me' became a real sacrifice of the ego to Christ. As he gave this expression in lectures, published as *Mysticism and Modern Thought* (1901) and *Christianity as Mystical Fact* (1902), his ethical individualism regained its rightful place.[22]

In the facts of nineteenth-century science he discovered spiritual impulses, and expressed them as ideas in a book on conceptions of the world and life in the nineteenth century, which was later incorporated in his *Riddles of Philosophy*.[23] In a short article he showed how the goal of philosophy has been to experience the world in ideal images, and how these await the experience by which the mind may step through into the world of spirit. He was now clear that his task was to lay a foundation for anthroposophy as an objective continuation of natural science, not something set beside it as subjective— to put life into the ideas of science so that they lay hold on the spiritual. He thus took the decision to break with tradition and publicize esotericism.[24] He attended a congress of the Theosophical Society in London in 1902, finding an inner content only among the English members. And he gained fresh insight from visits to the scientific museums there.

On return to Berlin the German Section of the Theosophical Society was founded with himself as General Secretary, on the clear understanding that he would promulgate only his own research. He even left the meeting to speak to non-theosophists on anthroposophy.[25] He was supported from the beginning by Marie von Sivers, who brought the arts of poetry and recitation into the work.[26] They at once established a monthly *Luzifer* (meaning only 'the light bringer')—soon combined into *Luzifer-Gnosis*—in which to publish basic anthroposophy. In contrast to the ancient dreamlike knowledge in the Society, he carried the experience of ideas in full clarity into the spiritual world through the will-to-knowledge, thinking like a mathematician but in pictures instead of figures. This was opposed by the leaders of the Society. 'I had of course a fully developed standing within the spiritual world; but I had in about 1902 and later imaginations, inspirations and intuitions.' The results were gradually brought together in his writings.[27]

PART SIX—FROM SPIRITUAL SCIENCE
(RELATED TO THE FOREGOING)

23. Historical Aspects

All philosophers before Aristotle were inspired by the wisdom of the mysteries. But Aristotle, the founder of logic, rightly distinguished matter and form (percept and concept). Medieval Scholasticism spoke more specifically of thoughts in terms of universals. The *universalia ante rem* (before the thing) is the pure spiritual form; the *universalia in re* (in the thing) is the form active in the sense world, for example as species; and the *universalia post rem* (after the thing) is the form that arises in our consciousness as concept. The element *ante* that reaches us from outer reality is of a purely spiritual nature, experienced as imprinted on us like a seal on wax; nothing of it passes over but its effect. Pure thought as an actual process is pure form, initially void of any particular content; yet it harmonizes with experience, and must first have been united with the *universalia ante rem.*

Then the Arabs brought a natural science and medicine saturated with Aristotelianism. But they made him appear as a foe of Christianity, so Scholasticism had to 'interpret' Aristotle's teaching as a basis for its conception of Christianity. It would have been natural to expand his technique of thinking (which is almost unaltered today) so as to grasp ever higher portions of the supersensible world. But instead there occurred a break in spiritual life; supersensible knowledge was ascribed to faith alone. Empirical science and an aversion to the technique of thinking then led to Kant's inability to grasp the 'thing in itself'. This is the break that must now be repaired.

Ever since the Middle Ages, most philosophers have been Nominalists, holding that general concepts are no more than names, and sound reasons have been adduced for this. Equally sound arguments, however, exist in favour of Realism, that concepts are part of reality. There is no justification for generalizing either view over the whole sphere of thinking. There are some concepts where Realism is correct and others where Nominalism. What matters is to know with which one is dealing.[1]

It was a peculiarity of Latin that the language itself shaped thinking. Despite the fact that hardly anyone learns Latin today, Latinized English sentences still enter the brain during education; consequently many people today simply cannot think.[2] So long as one restricts oneself to the intellect it is possible moreover to represent each thought by a word appropriately cut to shape by definitions, and then to replace thinking by a manipulation of words. This requires less effort than thinking, and consequently many people are satisfied with it. One thinks in words much more than one believes to be the case; and this is not realized, because one needs to adopt a mobile way of thinking before one can recognize the difference—it is a difference not proved but experienced.[3]

We have seen that the soul extinguishes at the first sight of things something of their reality, so that they appear to the senses in a form that is not full reality. Cognition adds back what makes the whole reality manifest—it is not that the soul adds anything unreal or unrelated. Our experience of being separated from the world is only a phenomenon of our consciousness. This must be overcome by understanding that at a certain stage a transient form of ego appears, because the forces connecting us with the world have been pressed outside consciousness. The forces which live in that part of reality withdraw and hide, in order to let the self-conscious ego shine brightly with its own light. *Otherwise the self-conscious ego would not come about.* Once this is admitted, one can no longer expect an answer to the riddles of philosophy in the experiences of normal ego-consciousness.[4]

Philosophy, love of wisdom, is not merely an affair of the intellect, but of the entire human soul. Wisdom was once considered something real, felt in warmth of soul—it was then experienced by the etheric body,* which not only gives life to the physical but drew ideas from the supersensible world. Knowledge has however become dry and cold; we no longer feel it to be in the midst of reality. We must first recover knowledge of the etheric human being, then philosophy will regain its character of reality.[5]

What the *Philosophy of Freedom* contains is absolutely necessary for anyone who seeks a secure foundation for spiritual knowledge. The attempt is made to show that a knowledge of the spirit realm *before* entry on actual spiritual knowledge is fully justified.[6]

Monism repairs the break in consciousness that relegated knowledge of the spirit to mere belief or disbelief.

24. Sense-perception and Thinking

When we see, the first event is actually the play of processes that permeate the eye with the ego and astral

---

* The etheric body is the totality of formative forces of life and growth, which distinguish the plant from the mineral and manifest in the living human being in many ways, especially in memory, thoughts and temperament. See further Rudolf Steiner's *Theosophy* or *Esoteric Science*.

organism.* You need only consider whether, when you see a red surface, you can distinguish your ego from this red. You cannot—it fills your consciousness completely. The red and the ego flow together—you must first separate them, and it is the same with the astral organism. The kidney system must also be considered; its fluid system is a living liquid that carries finely dissolved solid constituents throughout the organism, even up into the eyes. On its waves the etheric organism streams into the eye, filling it out, and also into the optic nerve. Into this flow the pictures that arise in the astral body, and that which arises through the ego. Thus there come together, in eye and nerve, from outside the impressions first in ego and astral body, and from inside the physical body borne on the mineral constituents and the etheric body borne on the fluid constituents.[7]

When for example we perceive yellow, yellow is enlivened in the eye by the object. Our etheric body penetrates this and drives out the outer life with its own inner life, leaving a dead yellow. So now there is an image of yellow enlivened from within, shot with a tinge of the corpse of yellow. Our astral body penetrates this inwardly enlivened yellow, and produces there an enlivened blue image, which in turn affects the etheric life-process and produces a blue physiological process in the eye but not beyond it.[†] All this remains unconscious. Now the life of the enlivened yellow is dulled by the ego,

---

*The astral body is the source of consciousness and movement that distinguishes the animal from the plant. In the human being it is highly complex, manifesting chiefly in sensation, feeling, aspiration and deed. The ego distinguishes humanity from the animal, and manifests primarily in walking, speaking and thinking. Ego and astral body are not spatial but work into space. See further Rudolf Steiner's *Theosophy* or *Esoteric Science*.
† The after-image.

which thus first acquires knowledge of it. The no longer living yellow now arises consciously in the astral body and over-shines the blue astral image, which remains unconscious. When the yellow object is removed, the overshining of the astral blue ceases, and it dies away to equilibrium.[8]

When we face a coloured object, a process of destruction takes place in the nervous system. Demolitions occur continuously and are made good again through the activity of the blood. Something is destroyed in both the physical and the etheric bodies. And since this destruction is caused in a quite specific path, a kind of 'channel' is bored into our organism from the eye to the cerebral cortex, and through this aperture slips the astral body in order to see the thing. Plato still saw this with atavistic clairvoyance; and through the new clair-voyance people must learn to know this channel, this tunnel through which the ego is united with that which works from outside. Mankind must learn not to form the sort of mental pictures usual in contemporary theory of knowledge or physiology, but learn to say: a channel, a tunnel is bored, and through this a door opens through which the astral body and ego step into connection with the outer world. This is a concept that the present does not have; hence it also does not know what follows from it as physiological fact.[9]

If we then want to perceive the thought 'lion', our thinking must first set in motion some part deep within the brain—we may if we wish say an atomistic portion—so that it becomes a mirror. The thought 'lion' can then be reflected, and the soul becomes conscious of it. The materialist finds it suits his purpose to say that the brain or central nervous system forms the thought; that is about as true as saying that a mirror makes the face. But the brain must be there first, then the soul-spiritual activity can make in it the appropriate little furrows,

its memoranda or engravings, and it then becomes conscious
of the reflected concept 'lion' corresponding to the percept.[10]

We are actually in the world of spirit when we have sense-
perceptions and ideas. It is the spiritual process in the physical
apparatus that we experience. The content of sense-
perceptions is definitely spiritual in nature; it is merely that
when we form ideas we extend the sensory activity to the
nerve organization, and nerve activity is actually a process of
dying—organic activity has to be excluded. Hence our life in
this sphere of the spirit is such that we have only images of it,
only a pale reflection.[11]

Because the human head is torn away from the horizontal
of the animal, and thus from the influence of the cosmos,
matter as such can there be reduced to dust, to nothing.
Imagine a painting where the physical substance turns to
dust, but where everything that was painted including the
nuances of colour remains in etheric form. Someone with
etheric perception could perceive this. And that is what the
thinking process is like.[12]

*Only through recognition of the reality of spirit can sense-
perception and thinking be understood.*

25. Pure Thinking

The concept of 'pure thinking'* is one we must be at pains to
acquire. We may look on it as an actual process which is pure
form, initially void of external content. To form the concep-

------

* Or 'sense-free thinking', 'body-free thinking'; 'higher thinking', 'living
thinking'.

tion of a circle we can construct in thought the sum of all places equidistant from one particular spot. No appeal to the senses is necessary; it is unquestionably a pure thought, yet it harmonizes with experience and is indeed indispensable for its comprehension. The activity apparently most subjective thus provides the very means for attaining reality in the most objective manner possible.[13]

Genuine thinking must always be willed; owing to its very nature it must appear to the observer as willed through and through. We forget that it is the 'I' itself which, from its standpoint inside thinking, observes its own activity. It is a clearly surveyable activity produced by the 'I' itself.[14]

When we grasp the 'I' in pure thinking we are in a centre where pure thinking produces its own essential substance. The 'I' lives within itself, produces its own concept, and lives therein as reality. If we now set to work at this point, cultivating our thinking so that it shall bear fruit and issue from itself, we then grasp the things of the world from within, which must eventually lead to anthroposophy.[15] We must raise ourselves into the ethereal realm of concepts if we would experience every aspect of existence. It is necessary to withdraw awhile from the immediate impressions of life, and to betake ourselves into the realm of pure thought. In the *Philosophy of Freedom* knowledge itself shall become organically alive, the ideas become powerful forces in life. One must be able to confront an idea and *experience* it; otherwise one will fall into its bondage.[16]

It is really impossible to *think* about thinking, but we can try to follow the path it indicates further, as in mathematics, where we arrive at the *beholding* of thinking. To do this we must already have an intensive conception of what pure, sense-free thinking is, and have pursued the inner work of thinking so far that we know that the thoughts are sense-free. In the *Philosophy of Freedom* I tried to lay thinking bare like mathematics, and have said that in such thinking we have the true communion of mankind, the union with true reality.[17]

The difficulty of grasping the essential nature of thinking by observing it is that it has all too easily eluded the intro-specting soul by the time we try to bring it to the focus of attention. Nothing then remains but the lifeless abstraction, the corpse of living thinking. If we only look at this, feeling and will appear in comparison so 'full of life'. But if we once succeed in really finding life in thinking, these cannot com-pare with the inner life and self-sustaining yet ever-moving *experience* of thinking. That thinking all too readily leaves us cold in recollection is nothing but the shadow of its real nature—warm, luminous and penetrating deeply into world phenomena. This penetration is brought about by a power flowing through thinking activity, the power of love in spiritual form. In the essence of thinking we find both feeling and will in the depth of their reality.[18]

The separation between percept and thought occurs only because we ourselves take up a position *in the midst of* exis-tence; nor is it otherwise in the case of spiritual perception. A difference only occurs to the extent that sense-perception reaches its consummation in reality through thought as it were in an upward direction at the beginning of the spiritual, whereas spiritual perception is experienced in its true being from this beginning downwards.[19]

Although intuitively experienced thinking is an active process taking place in the human spirit, it is also a spiritual percept grasped without a physical sense organ. It is a percept in which the perceiver is himself active, and a self-activity which is at the same time perceived. We are carried as perceiver into a spiritual world, within which whatever confronts us as percept in the same way will be recognized as a world of spiritual perception. This cannot appear as something foreign, because in intuitive thinking we already have a purely spiritual experience. A living comprehension of intuitive thinking will lead quite naturally to a living entry into the world of spiritual perception.[20]

A true judgement can only result when we have reached a certain maturity, when we have waited for the judgement to 'jump' to us; not when we put ourselves out to find it, but when we take pains to make ourselves ripe for it to come to us. Then the judgement we form will belong to reality. One who has learned wisdom, who has grown mature in the experience of life, will know that a general correctness of thought is of no significance at all, but that in each single case we have to give ourselves up to the facts as they present themselves and let them form the judgement. You may constantly find this confirmed in life.[21]

What matters is that we at least have the good will and effort to progress to thinking that is free of emotions such as we meet in life, and that we perceive how thoughts always grow out of one another and support one another. When we have got so far as to have a sequence of pure thoughts in our soul, then our mind is outside, the ego is outside—thence the rigour we feel in pure thinking. We cannot bend and break the thoughts as we subjectively would like—they cannot be otherwise. With our ego we are really not involved; thinking itself thinks. Only in this way does thinking become ripe to replace our own ego-content which we have emptied out. Instead of the content of our own mind, the content of mind of spirits of the higher Hierarchies must now enter into this free thinking. When you come to the point of having only the pure concepts as such, then the divine content enters, then you have the content from above.

No one could have thoughts and ideas, or even think abstractly, if they were not clairvoyant. In our ordinary thinking the pearl of clairvoyance is contained from the start. Ideas arise in the soul through exactly the same process as that which gives rise to its highest powers. It is immensely important to understand that clairvoyance begins in something common and everyday. We only have to recognize the supersensible nature of our concepts and ideas, and realize that these come to us from supersensible worlds; only then can we look at the matter rightly. The higher Hierarchies, from Seraphim down to Angels, must speak to the human soul from higher spiritual worlds. It is from those worlds that concepts and ideas come into the human soul, not from the world of the senses. 'O man, make bold to claim thy concepts and ideas as the beginning of thy clairvoyance'—I said this publicly in *Truth and Science* and the *Philosophy of Freedom*, where I showed that human ideas come from supersensible, spiritual knowledge.[23]

Try for once really to think actively and you will see how the heart is then engaged; then if one succeeds the whole human being enters with the greatest intensity into the spiritual world in a way suited to our modern age. For through active thinking we are able to bring force into our thinking, the force of a stout heart. If you do not seek the spirit on the path of thought, which although difficult to tread must be trodden with courage, with one's very heart's blood, you resemble an infant who believes he can draw nourishment out of himself, and not from his mother's breast. You only come to real content when you find the secret of developing within you an activity that enables you to draw again out of cosmic life the true spiritual nourishment. But this is pre-eminently a problem of the will experienced through thinking. Infinitely much depends on courageous, strong will, and no theories can solve what we need today.[24]

Sense-free thinking is already a clairvoyance in which higher Beings manifest.

26. *Cosmic Ether and Egohood*

It is of special significance to live in thoughts, spinning them out ever further, even as mere possibilities only. If you read the *Philosophy* rightly you must meet this fundamental tone or feeling that you are living, even if at first indefinitely, in the cosmos. This union with the cosmic secrets is the root-nerve of the *Philosophy*, where you find 'In thinking, we lift one corner of the veil of the cosmic secret' (p. 24). The implication is that when we really *experience* thinking we are no longer outside the divine essence but within it; we attain to the divine within ourselves.

For if we have really taken the trouble to acquire this experience of thinking, we are living in the etheric world. We then know that this world is not conditioned from any part of earthly space but by the whole cosmic sphere, and we can no longer doubt the order and reality of the cosmic etheric sphere. We reach what may be called etheric experience. Then we really make a noteworthy step forward in our whole life. We feel, quite rightly, that with our thinking we can grasp everything inwardly, that we are contacting the inner man, and we extend ourselves continually into our own being, we comprehend ourselves. This is a very important experience.

The result is that we break through our skin, and also grasp from within the entire cosmic ether—not in its details, naturally, but we gain the conviction that this ether is spread over the cosmic sphere within which we exist together with the stars, sun and moon and so on. Through this experience of thinking *a human being discovers his own self*, finds his bearings as an independent personality.[25]

The cosmic ether, which is common to all, carries within it the living thoughts in which we participate in the pre-earthly life before birth. They are never received from the cosmic ether between birth and death. No, the whole store of living thoughts is received at the moment when we come down from the spiritual world, from our own element of living thought, and form our etheric body. Within this ether body, the budding and organizing force in us, these living thoughts are still there.

If we consider the symptomatic life of thinking, feeling and willing, and behind it the real life of soul, then the thoughts constitute also part of the real life of soul. They build up our brain initially as an organ of demolition, gradually breaking down the living processes of nature and secreting matter all the time as nerves. And the nerves are thus endowed with a faculty resembling a mirror, which enables the thoughts of the surrounding ether to be reflected in them. (Section 24.) This is the organ of the superficial thinking in reflected pictures which we carry within us. This means that the thinking and forming of mental pictures in the superficial life of soul are the *reflection* of thoughts living in the cosmic ether. There cannot ever be in the cosmic ether a distorted, illogical or deranged thought, but the way the ether body with all its livingness will be depends on how we were able to receive it. Karma may not enable us to permeate the organism properly, so that here we may lack the formative thoughts of a properly developed etheric body.[26]

Things speak to us, and our inner nature speaks, when we observe them. These two languages originate from the same primal being, and we are called on to bring about their mutual understanding. That is what knowledge is. For one who does not understand this, things of the outer world remain alien. He does not hear their essence speaking out of his own inner nature, and therefore supposes that this essence is hidden behind the things. But when we reflect about them they cease to be outside us; we merge with their inner being. Our inner world *is* the inner aspect of nature.[27]

We shall arrive at a better conception of the ego from the point of view of the theory of knowledge by conceiving it as being itself within the law-conformity of things, and by viewing the bodily organization as only a sort of mirror that reflects back to the ego through the bodily activity its own living and moving outside the body in the so-called transcendental, namely, that part of the real world experienced as idea.[28]

The *percept* of the ego however is that of an entirely negative reality, and it is extremely important to recognize this. We do not have the ego in our consciousness, but only in our willing and in the feeling element that radiates from willing. When we perceive a fellow human being it is our willing that really does the perceiving, again as a negative reality. It is just because our ego is not in our consciousness, but outside it as our willing is, that we can enter the ego nature of the other. He claims our attention and puts us to sleep for a tiny moment, we reassert ourselves, and so it swings like a pendulum, falling asleep, waking in ourselves, as described in my *Philosophy of Freedom* (Appendix).[29]

The *Philosophy of Freedom* showed that all truly moral impulses have their origin in pure thinking, in which the will strikes into the otherwise passive realm of thought, stirring it awake and making the thinker inwardly active. If you read it correctly you come to realize that passive thinking was exactly like a corpse, the mere remains abandoned by what formerly indwelt it. You have to become aware of this by suffusing it with your own soul life, projecting your will into it, when searching for the source of moral impulses. Then you have the experience of being lifted by pure thinking out of your body and into a realm not of this earth. You realize that living thinking has no connection whatsoever with the physical world, although it is real, but rather with the spiritual world. You transcend the bounds of the planetary system.[30]

Pure thinking lifts the ego into the etheric world.

27. Moral Aspects

When we take into consciousness only what plays in from an instinctive reality, we cannot be free. Nothing which simply thrusts upwards out of our own corporeal, psychic or spiritual reality is alive there. But if we develop what I have called pure thinking, reality is there alive—although it is alive only in a mirrored image. As soon as we live in a reality we are under compulsion, for reality is something, and it works upon us no matter how weak it may be. It is an element of necessity, it constrains us and we must follow it. But when a mirrored image works upon our soul, such an image possesses no activity, no power over us.[31]

When we rise to truly free moral intuitions, we bring the

will into play to hasten matter transformed from our organism to the place where matter has been broken down (Section 24). We become inwardly creative, inwardly a builder. We see an empty place in the cosmos of the human organism filled out with quite new material construction. Purely moral deeds become a world-building element within us, right down into material substance. This is to discover the moral world as creative force.[32] The most real thought it is possible to hold is that the moral world order of today is the germinal force for the future order of nature. Morality is no mere worked-out thought; if permeated with reality it exists in the present as a germ for later external realities.[33]

The *Philosophy of Freedom* is in fact a picturing of morality intended to serve as a manual for enlivening dead thoughts by making them into moral impulses, for resurrecting them from the dead. In this sense there is indeed an inner content of Christianity in such a philosophy of freedom.[34]

On the basis of the two ideas that the unreality first presented to our senses is due to the way that we, not the world, are made, and that by our own effort we restore to the world the reality of which our perceiving deprived it, I call this a Pauline conception in the field of knowledge. For what is it if not carrying over into the realm of philosophy the Pauline idea that the human being in the person of Adam entered upon an inferior experience of the world, and only comes to experience it as it is through Christ's influence on him?* It is possible to find a bridge from this way of philosophizing to Christ, just as one can find a bridge from natural science to the Father. The natural-scientific way of thinking however cannot find the way to Christ.[35]

---

* I Cor. 15:45–9.

Since knowing is a real process, moral behaviour appears as the outcome of that which the individual experiences in a real process through moral fantasy and intuition. There results the ethical individualism which in fact is built on the Christ-impulse in us. For it is built on the spiritual activity we achieve by changing ordinary thinking into pure thinking, which rises to the spiritual world and there produces the stimulus to moral behaviour. The impulse to love, otherwise bound to the physical, becomes spiritualized. And the moral ideals borrowed from the spiritual world through moral imagination become forces of spiritual love. The transformed ego has developed into spheres of spirituality, and up there begins to love virtue—and hence practises virtue because it loves it of its own individuality. We laid stress on the transformation of the soul and on the real installation of the Christ impulse into it, even in thought life.[36]

The greater the strength and intensity of the inner radiation of will into the sphere of thinking, the more spiritual we become. It is possible to attain complete freedom in our inner life if we increasingly exclude the actual thought content from outside, and kindle into greater activity the element of will. Thereby *our thinking becomes pure thinking, which may equally be called pure will.** We thus prepare ourselves for moral imagination, which rises to moral intuitions that then illumine our will-thought. Everything that can stream from the spiritual world has its foundation in moral intuitions. Thus freedom dawns when our will becomes an ever mightier force in our thinking.

On the other side (outwards) our actions stream from our

---

* Will is the idea conceived as force—Section 15.

will, and we permeate them with thoughts. We perfect our actions by developing devotion to the outer world, which is nothing else but love. We attain love by permeating the life of will with thoughts. And because we are a unified whole, where we find freedom in the life of thought and love in the life of will, there will be freedom in our actions and love in our thinking. Thus the two great ideals of freedom and love grow together for the good of the world.[37]

People today simply study the laws at work in the world that can also be embodied in technological constructions—but moral laws are not found there. The mission of the *Philosophy of Freedom* was to show that the human being must therefore get out of himself. This first going beyond our self takes place in pure thinking. We leave the body entirely and transport our self into the outer world. We thus exercise the very first and subtlest function of clairvoyance, and come to possess moral intuitions, moral imagination. We depart from the ground of our self to discover the spirit in this first realm, the moral realm within the sphere of technology, for there the spirit is nonetheless to be found. That is the first stage of modern clairvoyance.[38]

It is nonsense to ask about the freedom of the will—it is only of the freedom of thoughts that we can speak. I drew the line very clearly in my *Philosophy of Freedom*. We must become free in our thoughts, and the free thoughts must give the impulse to the will—then we are free. With our thoughts we live in the mineral world; in all the rest of our being, with which we live in the plant, animal and human kingdoms, we are subject to destiny.[39]

Only a truly Christian Monism leads beyond freedom to love.

28. Self-knowledge

The essential thing is the inner education we must bestow on ourselves. Conquests must be made of which there is generally no inkling. The spiritual labour that this involves comes about in the inner being. Moral commandments can be grasped only in this realm, free from external impressions, resting upon inner human work itself. When we penetrate more intimately into this content we fit ourselves into the outer world of the senses. An advance thus occurs into the realm of pure spirituality—concept and idea are then transformed into image, into Imagination.[40]

On the path to its inner being the soul must press on beyond normal consciousness and get beneath its own surface. Instead of trying to think correctly, we can instead look mentally at the activity of thinking as such. We can place something like a symbolic picture (the object depicted is of no concern) into the centre of our consciousness, and go on holding it in mind, becoming completely absorbed in the inner soul-activity taking place. If such inner exercise is repeated long enough the soul will recognize experiences that detach it from ordinary thinking bound to physical organs. The same can be done with feeling, willing and even sensation. By such inner labour self-knowledge must first be uncovered, and then these activities become 'substantial' in a spirit sense, and first reveal their true inner nature. An unlimited intensification is meant of attentiveness and loving devotion to what is experienced in the soul, to such a degree that they are like entirely new soul forces.

One can thus seize a reality that reveals itself as independent of physical organs. This is a real experience of spiritual life. It brings recognition that even normal soul life is not produced by the body, but takes place outside it. I am as a self-conscious ego connected with colour, sound, etc. outside the body, the function of which can be compared with a mirror making the perception conscious. Whilst we sleep this reflection is interrupted; the ego lives only in the weaving activity of soul and spirit, so sleep is unconscious. But through these exercises and others, sleep experiences can be reflected within themselves, and thus become spiritual perceptions of a world in which the soul has its true life and being. There is no theoretical proof for the reality of such experiences, but neither is there for those of the sense world; only experience can decide in either case. Such experiences are as clear as those of mathematics (unless one is inclined to a nebulous mysticism). The very ideas of scientific thinking are the best on which to dwell in order to detach inner experience from the body. In this way spiritual science is the necessary continuation of natural-scientific thinking.

By penetrating into this reality inaccessible to the senses the soul experiences its inner and deeper being. Here appears a higher soul-spiritual individuality who stands to the body as to an instrument. Soul and spirit appear like the seed of a new plant, the germ for a future new individuality. The spiritual scientist investigates how this unfolds and recognizes it in heredity. Many problems of life and destiny then appear in a new light.[41]

In self-knowledge we ourselves stand within the object, weaving in creative activity the self which we inwardly observe. If we fail to realize the significance of this, all our knowledge is in a higher sense but blindness. To listen only to the voice within calls for a new sense that unites with the object and gathers it wholly into itself. Thus self-perception implies self-awakening. The thing confronting me is no longer separated from me; what I gather from it becomes part of myself. In awakening, I thus also awaken to a higher plane whatever I have made part of me from the world outside. A spiritual replica of the object is within me, and I gather from this infinitely more than from the outside object; there shines forth towards it what it really is. The outer fact is enrolled in the spiritual content already within me, causing the outer world to arise as spiritual entity on a higher plane. This is nothing but the result of inner experience, the faculty for which is common to all humanity.

The entire world reveals itself thus within us, the cosmic process confronts its own spiritual being, and our inner life and experience are enrolled within the objective world process. We find the things of the world endowed with new life, and a light shines forth as a sun revealing further knowledge of them, uniting us with the whole world. The entire world reveals itself within us, and our circumscribed individuality is enrolled within the great cosmic whole. Only such life dominated by this inner sense can uplift the human being above himself to say 'I am a general, universal "I"'. The isolated ego becomes absorbed in such moments by the universal ego. There is at this level no difference between Plato and myself; what separates us belongs at a lower level, whilst the universal principle active within us is one and the same. This cannot be proved, it can only be experienced. We all grasp one and the same idea, which is only there once. Separate truth is here merged into universal truth, identical in all. This exaltation of the individual to the universal ego is the secret revelation in the inmost heart, the root mystery of life. If our highest goal be called the divine, we may say that the divine is not reproduced in the soul as external image, but is awakened in us. Self-knowledge signifies the capacity to live and work within the innermost kernel of the world that comes to life as spiritual being.

When a motive is comprehended in self-knowledge, it becomes part of the self. The will is no longer determined; it determines itself. Only such action is free whose every detail is aglow with self-observation and flows from the universal self. Our deeds become deeds of universal being. We fail to be human in the highest sense if we do not unfold our being to join the universal self. Not poorer but fuller, richer, is that life which is restored to us in the spirit.[42]

Philosophy culminates in self-knowledge, which is also world-knowledge.

PART SEVEN—BIOGRAPHICAL (42–64)

29. Foundations of Anthroposophy (1903–9)

From now onwards, Steiner's life is inextricably bound up with that of the Anthroposophical Movement, and first with the establishment of basic facts concerning the spiritual world. Whilst he himself undertook the writing of books and articles for *Luzifer Gnosis* and lecture tours throughout Europe, Marie von Sivers made all the necessary arrangements. His style of writing was deliberately dry, to stimulate readers' own will to supply the warmth. He took great care to speak only from his own experience, and only to say what his audience was ready to understand.

In *Knowledge of the Higher Worlds*, first published serially, the new western Christian-Rosicrucian path of initiation was made publicly available for the first time. *Cosmic Memory*, also serialized, sketched episodes from the spiritual evolution of the world and of humanity. *Theosophy* leads from subtle observations of the human being to reincarnation and body-free ideas of life in the soul world and spiritland after death. His thinking, in extending beyond the sense world, combines the precision of mathematics with a mobile and pictorial quality. For those already experienced in spiritual matters he formed his own esoteric school within that of the Theosophical Society, and also conducted meetings in the field of Freemasonry, both based on his own research. He said of the period 1901–8: 'I stood with all my soul forces under the influence of facts and Beings of the spiritual world that came towards me.'[1]

The second period in the life of the Anthroposophical Movement began in 1907 with the great lecture cycles on the Gospels, Genesis and the Apocalypse; and the true Christian mysteries open up, culminating in the prediction of the imminent appearance from 1933 onwards of Christ in the etheric world to a few individuals. In contrast the Theosophical Society put forward an Indian boy, Krishnamurti, as a physical reincarnation of Christ, which was rejected by Steiner and followers as impossible. He described his entry into the Society until 1907 as a martyrdom, each step a battle against its traditions which he had hoped to redeem and Christianize.[2]

Through Marie von Sivers, art was becoming a modern experience of the spirit, but at the Society congress in Munich in 1907 the introduction of drama, recitation, colour and occult seals met much opposition. In 1908 *Luzifer Gnosis* folded simply because Steiner's work left him no time to write for it. He did however complete his *Occult Science, an Outline* (1910) restating the work hitherto and extending the spiritual view of world evolution back to ancient Saturn. But his lectures on manifestations of karma did not find a reception on which he could build.

30. Artistic Creativity (1910–16)

The early part of this period saw the creation of four Mystery Dramas, which provide practical examples of the working of reincarnation and karma in a group of people over four incarnations, including scenes between death and rebirth. It was noted that audiences departed in silence. Innumerable insights into the spiritual and soul worlds are portrayed, especially the battle in each soul between the opposing powers and the forces of Christ.

In 1912 a site was offered on the Dornach hill near Basle for a suitable building for the dramas and related work. After visiting it Steiner appeared 'haggard, crushed and sombre', but he decided to build. His architectural design, conceived not on a drawing board but with a three-dimensional model, was not only highly original, but with its self-supporting intersecting domes of different sizes 'required mathematical genius of a high order'.

The year 1912 also saw the birth of an entirely new art of movement—eurythmy—through which both music and speech are given objective colourful expression. A soul Calendar was also published, making it possible to participate in the transformation of the soul week by week through the year.

Early in 1913 the German section of the Theosophical Society was dissolved and the Anthroposophical Society founded 'because we had to'. Steiner was its teacher, but not a member. It had at first twelve 'sectlike little groups' meeting for his lectures and study. The Western esoteric school inspired through him was now independent, though still in harmony with the Eastern school.

In September the foundation stone of the Goetheanum building—two interpenetrating copper dodecahedra a yard long—was laid. This was a mystery deed in which the spiritual Hierarchies were invoked by name and the origin of the Lord's Prayer was revealed. Steiner united his etheric body fully with that of the Goetheanum: 'It was one of the most sublime moments of my experience.'

His *Riddles of Philosophy* gives remarkable insights into the whole course of the development of philosophic thought from

Pherekydes to Einstein, and especially that of the nineteenth century.

Steiner's removal from Berlin to Dornach began a new period in the life of the Society. As a widower he now married Marie von Sivers. At the start of the War the esoteric school was closed, but people from 17 nations continued to work harmoniously together on the wooden building, forming a real community. He himself worked actively with them, tirelessly sculpturing the capitals and architraves, painting the small cupola and directing the whole. He invented new techniques of glass engraving and stage lighting; and he produced and acted in dialect the Oberufer Christmas plays.

His lectures were restricted by war to German-speaking countries, which determined the shape of the Society. He spoke of evil as the misuse of spiritual forces for egotistic ends, and the forces of life in art as a balance to those of destruction. In 1915 came the first eurythmy course, and in 1916 a course on the history of art (with 700 slides) and the production of some scenes from Goethe's *Faust*. Important indications were also given concerning the twelve senses.

31. Social Creativity (1917–23)

In 1917 Rudolf Steiner was asked to advise on the reconstruction of Germany once the war was over, and emphasized the importance of separating the spiritual, political and economic spheres so that they can mutually negotiate—the Threefolding of the Social Order. The leaders had no organ, time or strength with which to grasp such a possibility. He put much energy into developing these ideas for the rest of this period, but without success. He also published the result of 30 years' research on the threefolding of the human body (on which his social ideas were based); and he spoke of the 33-year rhythm deriving from the life of Jesus Christ.

In 1919 he spoke of the 'temporary ending' of the war, seeing it in the context of the great battle between the opposing powers and Christ. Now spiritual impulses could again be brought into practical life. After lectures on pedagogy and the training of teachers (sometimes even overnight) the first Waldorf school was opened with 15 teachers and 200 pupils.

At Michaelmas 1920 the Goetheanum building could be brought into use with courses in the sciences and arts, though it was never 'opened' or consecrated further. Meanwhile the influx of new members unfortunately brought with them habits of the world which lacked esoteric substance and were not easily transformed. As he had predicted, these two facts caused an intensification of attacks and calumnies. These were calmly corrected, but the opposition became deliberately orchestrated, including a warning of arson. This caused Steiner severe battles, waste of energy and unspeakable suffering, and may be seen as part of the battle between the Archangel Michael and the dragon in social life.

Research was undertaken on healing by means of etheric forces and life rhythms, and a course on spiritual science and medicine led to the opening in 1921 of a clinic with Dr Ita Wegman, followed by a course on curative eurythmy. From this developed the discipline of anthroposophical medicine.

By 1922 Steiner was attracting large audiences in Germany (over 20,000 in one fortnight), and receiving streams of visitors bringing their problems. His tours included Stratford, Oxford and London. Work in Dornach included courses on drama and economics, and a course for young people. In

Stuttgart he gave rituals for the Christian Community, founded by Dr Rittlemeyer alongside the Society. And for farmers he advised the biodynamic farming methods and preparations. But he thought the Society itself 'lacked inner stability, somewhat resembling a ruin'.

This phase of the Society's work culminated on the last night of 1922 in the fire that destroyed the Goetheanum. For Steiner it was not only a tragedy but tore his etheric body, such that he wrote 'Since January 1923 my higher members are not fully united with my physical body. I lost when living in spiritual realms direct connection with my physical organization—not however with the physical world, where the possibility of sound judgement was stronger and more comprehensive.' The work continued next day in the carpenter's workshop without interruption. The opposition behind the arson he ascribed to the daughters (the practical activities) forgetting their mother (the esoteric centre) and to the membership not being sufficiently inwardly awake.

During 1923 separate regional societies were founded, with a second in Germany for the younger element. These were then all brought together at the Christmas Foundation in a newly formed Anthroposophical Society, which can be felt as a metamorphosis of the lost building, vehicle of the Being Anthroposophia, the two domes, stage and auditorium becoming the School of Spiritual Science and the Society. Steiner, in taking on the presidency of an esoteric society, risked the withdrawal of his inspiration, whereas it proved to be enhanced. He also took responsibility for the deeds of members as his own karma (as did Christ for all people). The effect right into his physical body, the seat of karma, was a severe and sudden illness like a swordthrust, outwardly due to poison.

Lecture work nevertheless continued at high intensity in many fields, including a conference at Penmaenmawr.

32. *Final Years (1924–5)*

The words inspired by Michael began to flow through Rudolf Steiner directly into the School of Spiritual Science with its professional Sections. And in the Society came a long series of lectures, published later under the title *Karmic Relationships*, in which many examples of the relationship between successive lives of public characters can be studied. The ahrimanic beings, who had for so long prevented this, were silenced. The cosmos was open to Steiner, and a greater flow of inspiration poured from him.

At Whitsun the Biodynamic agricultural movement was founded. His last visit abroad was to Torquay and Tintagel, where he experienced the school of Arthur. In September he was giving four different courses of lectures daily, which he affirmed was possible despite his impaired health. But the extra demand for an average of 20 private interviews daily overtaxed his strength. At Michaelmas he had to take to his bed, placed at the foot of the statue of Christ as he saw him clairvoyantly, which he was carving and had almost completed. He described his illness as that of the Society, his physical body being no longer his own. Had each member from the different esoteric streams healed their karma, he could have recovered. But it was not to be. Meanwhile he continued his weekly letters to members (which were to be eventually published as *Anthroposophical Leading Thoughts*), and he also wrote his autobiography.

When his life drew to an early close, he felt his work

unfinished. He took no goodbyes, and nominated no successor as leader of the School. He continued his work from the spiritual world, through those with the ears to hear.

Epilogue

The foregoing is only an introductory skeleton of Rudolf Steiner's philosophy. The next task is to transform the soul so that this has organic life. That means to work through the original works, especially the *Philosophy of Freedom,* itself a living organism in a real environment, struggling with all the forms of opposition there described and the way to rebut them. The objective is to bring that organism as much to life within as does a professional musician who is to perform by heart a concert of piano sonatas. We need to become no less professional in our thinking in the context of the environment of today, if we are to represent adequately the foundation on which anthroposophy (spiritual science) is built.

> The rich fullness of matter
> Penetrates human senses
> Full of riddles from world depths.
> The spirit's clarifying word
> Streams into grounds of soul
> Full of content from world heights
> They meet in human inwardness
> For fuller wisdom of reality.

> Rudolf Steiner
> (translated by the editor)

Appendix
Rudolf Steiner's Inner Life

For those familiar with anthroposophical terminology, it seems possible to interpret the course of Rudolf Steiner's inner development in relation to his outer life in the following terms:

Childhood (0–7) Section 1 (1861–7)

Like many children Rudolf Steiner was aware of the elemental nature beings, but he was equally full of wonder at the sub-natural beings in everything mechanical brought about by human work.

Boyhood (7–14) Section 2 (1868–74)

During the time of Mercury's influence the soul gradually awakens to find itself between the sense world and the inner world of the spirit. As his etheric body develops he feels joy that the soul light of his own thinking can grasp the inner world, at first in geometry. An ability to perceive souls of the deceased in the soul world he cultivates alone.

Youth (14–21) Section 3 (1875–81)

As the astral body develops he gains an outstanding active soul force, the Venus influence, expressed in his exceptional power of self-development. In 1879, he received spiritual guidance from someone whose advice suggests that he was an incarnation of Christian Rosencreutz. This was also the year when Michael, already Archon for the whole cultural age, became the ruling Archangel of Time. During this time the demands of Steiner's karma—to resolve the relationship between sense world and spiritual world necessarily severed by the theology of Thomas Aquinas—are fully established.

Vienna (21–28) Section 4 (1882–8)

Now when the ego, working with the soul life forces of the sun, normally develops the sentient soul, Steiner's work on Goethe's idea of the archetypal plant enables him to recreate in the mind the life-processes of nature. This raised his thinking to the condition of Imagination, and not only marked the successful outcome of a battle with Lucifer (through whom comes intellectual thinking) but also wrecked Ahriman's aim to allow only dead thoughts to exist. Like Schionatulander in the Grail story, he prepares the way for the Parzival initiation.

Weimar (28–35) Section 21 (1889–95)

When Michael was beginning to take incisive hold of the Cosmic Intelligence again on earth, Steiner tells that his intellectual soul, which is normally developed at this age, was still held in the spiritual world. He says that he lived in lower spiritland among Michael and his opponents. He felt great inner loneliness at this time, which is the essential precondition for the capacity of Inspiration, and so he was probably already developing this. By finalizing his *Philosophy of Freedom*, the basic problems of philosophy that have existed since Aristotle are resolved.

Berlin (35–42) Section 22 (1896–1902)

At the age when the consciousness soul normally develops, he awakens to a new awareness of the reality of the sense world, and undergoes severe tests, both inner and outer—he 'enters the skin of the dragon'. This, and his penetration into a wide variety of other minds, including those of the proletariat, point to the development of Intuition. With this his sun-initiation instigated by the Rosencreutz figure is completed. This is crowned by the full sacrifice of his ego to Christ. He already speaks out concerning anthroposophy, with insight similar to that of the Greek Mysteries.

Foundations of anthroposophy (42–9) Section 29 (1903–9)
We see here the new Age of Light streaming in after the end of
Kali Yuga. He forms his own esoteric school and speaks there
of inspiration from the Masters, especially Christian Rosencreutz and Jesus of Nazareth. He is also reported as
acknowledging it from the Maitreya Bodhisattva, 'the bringer
of good through the Word in the service of Christ', receiving
therewith the collective wisdom known as the Holy Spirit.
Through his astral body transformed to Anthropos-Sophia
he receives the Spirit Self. The Michael-impulse thus enters
the realm of knowledge. He is at the age ruled by Mars and
Spirits of Movement, masters of the Cosmic Word; and one
may feel he has reached the stage of 'living in the relationship
between Macrocosm and Microcosm'.

Artistic Creativity (49–56) Section 30 (1910–16)
This age is influenced by Jupiter and the Spirits of Wisdom,
and one may feel that he is 'becoming one with the Macrocosm'. From the intimate Gospel cycles and the announce-
ment of Christ's appearance in the etheric, one feels special
inspiration from the Master Jesus. The Michael-impulse
flows into the life of feeling and the arts—the first Mystery
Dramas were specifically given 'through' Steiner. That he not
only designs the Goetheanum building but unites his etheric
body with it suggests the beginning of transforming the
etheric body to Life Spirit.

Social Creativity (56–63) Section 31 (1917–23)
These years are ruled by Saturn and the Spirits of Will, and
from this derive the many practical social initiatives—medi-
cal, educational, agricultural, etc. One feels here, especially in
the reforming of the Anthroposophical Society as both public
and esoteric, the direct influence of Michael in the will. His
separation from his physical body, and its dependence on the

karma of Society members, suggests the beginning of its transformation to Spirit Man.

Final Years (63–4) Section 32 (1924–5)

The soul is now free in the cosmos. The Michael-impulse works directly through him, creating the School of Spiritual Science in the service of Christ for mankind's future.

References

A = Autobiography, and is followed by chapter number
Where book or lecture dates are given, see Bibliography for titles

Part One
1. A1 and 4.2.13
2. 4.2.13
3. A1
4. A2 and 4.2.13
5. A2
6. A3
7. 4.2.13
8. A3
9. 4.2.13
10. A3
11. A5
12. A6
13. A7
14. 10.6.23
15. A7
16. 4.2.13
17. 11.6.23
18. A8
19. A9
20. A13

Part Two
1. 86/3
2. 86/4
3. 86/5
4. 86/7
5. 92/4
6. 94/3
7. 94/4
8. 86/8
9. 86/9
10. 86/10
11. 86/12
12. 86/11
13. 86/13
14. 87/9
15. 94/4
16. 91/16/2
17. 91/16/3
18. 91/15
19. 94/5
20. 94/6
21. 86/13
22. 86/11
23. 92/Pr
24. 87/7
25. 94/6
26. 86/12
27. 94/7
28. 92/8

Part Three
1. 87/10/1
2. 86/11
3. 87/10/3
4. 87/10/2
5. 86/13
6. 91/16/1
7. 91/16/2
8. 91/16/5
9. 91/17/4
10. 87/10/4
11. 92/5
12. 87/6
13. 85/4
14. 86/15
15. 87/10/3
16. 86/15
17. 91/15/1
18. 91/17/2
19. 91/17/5
20. 91/15/1
21. 94/7
22. 91/17/3
23. 85/1
24. 85/2
25. 86/16
26. 85/4
27. 86/16
28. 87/10/5

29. 85/4
30. 85/3
31. 94/9
32. 86.13
33. 94/8
34. 92/6
35. 94/2
36. 86/17
37. 91/16/3
38. 86/17

Part Four
1. 86/17
2. 86/18
3. 86/19
4. 87/10/5
5. 92/8
6. 94/12
7. 87/10/5
8. 94/9
9. 94/13
10. 94/1
11. 94/9
12. 94/12
13. 94/9
14. 86/18
15. 87/10/5
16. 86/17
17. 94/9
18. 94/10
19. 94/14
20. 86/21
21. 87/8
22. 87/10/5

23. 88
24. 91/16/4
25. 91/16/6
26. 94/P2
27. 86/14
28. 86/13
29. 87/6
30. 87/9
31. 87/10/5
32. 87/10/3
33. 91/17/8
34. 94/10
35. 94/15

Part Five
1. A11
2. A14
3. A10
4. A14
5. 3.8.24
6. A16
7. A17
8. A18
9. A20
10. A22
11. A23
12. A17
13. A25
14. A27
15. A26
16. A27
17. A30
18. A28
19. A27

20. A30
21. A26
22. A27
23. A30
24. A31
25. A30
26. A31
27. A32

Part Six
1. 08
2. 28.6.23
3. 20.1.14
4. 14/17
5. 6.9.22
6. 18/Preface
7. 20.10.22
8. Précis of letter from Rudolf Steiner to W.J. Stein
9. 2.4.18
10. 23.1.14
11. 4.11.21
12. 30.10.21
13. 08
14. 18/3
15. 08
16. 18/Preface of 94 revised
17. 30.9.20
18. 18/8
19. 24/4
20. 18/5

21. 27.12.11
22. 14.9.15
23. 29.5.13
24. 10.10.22
25. 23.11.23
26. 26.6.24
27. 97/18
28. 11
29. 5.10.19

30. 6.2.23
31. 28.12.18
32. 30.8.21
33. 27.2.17
34. 2.4.22
35. 4.9.17
36. 24.5.20
37. 19.12.20
38. 7.5.22

39. 17.2.24
40. 30.9.20
41. 14/17
42. 01/1

Part Seven
1. A33
2. 14.6.23

Bibliography

Written Works

1885   *Goethe the Scientist/Nature's Open Secret*—1 to 5
1886   *Theory of Knowledge Implicit in Goethe's World
        Conception/The Science of Knowing*
1887   *Goethe the Scientist/Nature's Open Secret*—6 to 14
1888   *Goethe as Father of a New Aesthetics*
1891   *Goethe the Scientist/Nature's Open Secret*—15 to 17
1892   *Truth and Science*
1894   *Philosophy of Spiritual Activity/Philosophy of Freedom/
        Intuitive Thinking as a Spiritual Path*
1897   *Goethe the Scientist/Nature's Open Secret*—18
1901   *Mysticism and Modern Thought/Mysticism at the Dawn of
        the Modern Age/Mysticism after Modernism*
1908   *Philosophy and Anthroposophy*
1911   *Psychological Foundations of Anthroposophy*
1914   *Riddles of Philosophy*
1918   Addenda to *Philosophy of Freedom*
1924   Addenda to *Theory of Knowledge/The Science of Knowing*
1924–5 Autobiography *The Course of My Life*

Lectures

GA = *Gesamtausgabe* (Collected Edition)

9.2.05   Not translated. GA53 *Grundbegriffe der Theosophie*
27.12.11 *World of the Senses and World of the Spirit*—1
4.2.13   *Self-Education: Autobiographical Reflections*
29.5.13   *Occult Foundations of the Bhagavad Gita*—2

The above titles are available through the book trade or from www.rudolfsteinerpress.com (UK) or www.steinerbooks.org (USA).

Out-of-print titles can be found in specialist libraries, such as the Rudolf Steiner Library at 35 Park Rd., London NW1 6XT.